Acclaim for the Book

JONATHAN KOZOL
AUTHOR, "ORDINARY RESURRECTIONS"

This is a beautiful book of surpassing dignity and tenderness...I hope it will be widely read, not only by those who call themselves religious. Although written with great simplicity of style, it is nonetheless a work of moral mystery...a small treasure, unpretentious and transcendent.

CICELY SAUNDERS
FOUNDER, ST. CHRISTOPHER'S HOSPICE, LONDON

There are many books available by people bereaved of someone they loved, but this one has a special strength.

FR. BENEDICT GROESCHEL, C.F.R.
ARCHDIOCESE OF NEW YORK

Engaging and challenging. I found myself saying "yes" chapter after chapter. A witness to the power of faith.

PAUL BRAND, M.D.
AUTHOR, "PAIN: THE GIFT NOBODY WANTS"

I have read many books about dying, but this is the one I would give to someone approaching death or facing bereavement. From start to finish it shines with hope! I want a copy beside my bed when my time comes.

WILLIAM DONAHUE
PRESIDENT, CATHOLIC LEAGUE
FOR RELIGIOUS AND CIVIL RIGHTS

Each page of *Be Not Afraid* is touched with a poignant reality and an open expression of love's power to overcome suffering and death...it traces our fears to a basic source: a soul starved of love. This is a wonderful book.

JOHN DEAR, S.J.
AUTHOR, "THE GOD OF PEACE"

Arnold challenges me to confront my own fear of death...his stories encourage me to embrace the God of life. They are a great comfort.

MILTON W. HAY
NATIONAL COUNCIL OF HOSPICE PROFESSIONALS

This book is an extraordinarily helpful clinical and inspirational resource. To open oneself to it is to come upon an almost unbearably widened vista of living.

MARY E. O'BRIEN, M.D.
OVERLAKE SENIOR HEALTH CTR., BELLEVUE, WA.

This book should be required reading for anyone in the healthcare professions and for anyone in search of the answers to life's most baffling questions.

REV. WILLIAM GROSCH, M.D.
CAPITAL DISTRICT PSYCHIATRIC CTR., ALBANY, N.Y.

This gem of a book speaks volumes about God's love and made me cry tears of sadness, but also of joy. I commend it to all those in the helping professions.

VERNON GROUNDS
DENVER SEMINARY, DENVER, CO.

This book is a wonderful witness to how the fear of dying need not have the final word. It stirs, even awakens, the soul.

Be Not Afraid

OTHER TITLES BY THE AUTHOR

Escape Routes: For People Who Feel Trapped in Life's Hells

Endangered: Your Child in a Hostile World

Why Forgive? (British title: The Lost Art of Forgiving)

Seeking Peace: Notes and Conversations along the Way

Cries from the Heart: Stories of Struggle and Hope

Sex, God, and Marriage

Drained: Stories of People Who Wanted More

Be Not Afraid

OVERCOMING THE FEAR OF DEATH

Johann Christoph Arnold

ORBIS BOOKS
Maryknoll, New York 10545

Sixth Printing, May 2008

Founded in 1970, Orbis Books endeavors to publish works that enlighten the mind, nourish the spirit, and challenge the conscience. The publishing arm of the Maryknoll Fathers and Brothers, Orbis seeks to explore the global dimensions of the Christian faith and mission, to invite dialogue with diverse cultures and religious traditions, and to serve the cause of reconciliation and peace. The books published reflect the views of their authors and do not represent the official position of the Maryknoll Society. To learn more about Maryknoll and Orbis Books, please visit our website at www.maryknoll.org.

ORBIS/ISBN 1-57075-511-6

The Library of Congress has cataloged the original edition as follows:

Library of Congress Cataloging–in-Publication Data

Arnold, Johann Christoph 1940-
    Be not afraid: overcoming the fear of death / Johann Christoph Arnold.
        p. cm.
Includes index.
    ISBN 0-87486-916-1 (pbk.: alk. paper)
    1. Death—Religious aspects—Bruderhof Communities. 2. Bruderhof Communities—Doctrines. 1. Title.
    BT825.A69 2002
    248.8'6—dc21
                                                    2001007429

God is love; and he who abides in love abides in God.
In this we may have confidence on the day of judgment...
There is no fear in love; perfect love casts out fear.

1 JOHN 4:16–18

Contents

Foreword xi

Introduction xiv

1

Foundations 1

2

Fear 12

3

Despair 22

4

Losing a Baby 33

5

Reverence 41

6

The Childlike Spirit 48

7

Anticipation 59

8

Readiness 67

9

Accidents 77

10

Beyond Medicine 86

11

In God's Hands 94

12

Suffering 105

13

Faith 118

14

Courage 128

15

Healing 140

16

Caring 150

17

Dying 160

18

Grief 171

19

Resurrection 187

Epilogue 197

Index 203

Foreword
by Madeleine L'Engle

One evening while my children were doing homework, I was sitting at my desk writing, when one of our neighbors, a young man in high school, came in demanding, "Madeleine, are you afraid of death?"

Barely turning, I answered, "Yes, Bob, of course." He plunked himself down on a chair. "Thank God. Nobody else will dare to admit it."

Death is change, and change is always fearful as well as challenging, but until we can admit the fear, we cannot accept the challenge. Until we can admit the fear, we cannot know the assurance, deep down in our hearts, that indeed, we are *not* afraid.

Be Not Afraid is a wonderful book about the kind of fearlessness of death that comes despite the normal fears we have, no matter how deep our faith. Indeed, it is only deep faith that can admit fear, and then move on to the understanding that God can work through our tragedies as well as our joys; that even when accidents and illness let us down, God never lets us down.

I am also grateful that *Be Not Afraid* addresses the paradox of our abuse of the great gift of free will, and God's working out of Love's plan for the universe. No, God does not cause or will the death of a child, but God can come into all things, no matter how terrible. God can help us to bear them, and even be part of them.

In a society that is afraid of death – not the normal fear Bob expressed, but the terrible fear that surrounds us when we are not centered on God – we tend to isolate the dying, implying that death is contagious. Yes, we all die; there are no exceptions; but we are not meant to die alone. I was taken through a beautiful new cancer hospital where in each room there was what looked like a small mahogany table. In a moment it could be pulled out and turned into a bed, where a family member or friend could be with the person who was ill.

I was privileged to be with my husband, holding him, at the time of his death. The grace to be with other people as they have made the great transition has been given me. Perhaps when I answered Bob's question with,

"Yes, of course," I was referring to awe, rather than fear or panic, an awe some of us are afraid to face.

I wish a friend had put this beautiful book in my hands when my husband died. It honors life, and in honoring life it honors death. It also honors the One who made us all with such love. God came to live with us as Jesus, to show us how to live, and to die, and that gives us assurance of the Resurrection, and of life in eternity – that is, of life beyond time and all that is transient, in God's love forever.

Goshen, Connecticut

Introduction
by the Author

Are you afraid of dying? Do you know someone who is? Have you ever wondered how you would survive the loss of someone you love? Whether consciously or not, every life is sooner or later touched by death, and thus every person must deal with these questions at one point or another. That is why I have written this book.

We cannot avoid death. It overshadows all our lives. We live longer than our grandparents; we are better fed; we lose fewer babies. Vaccines protect us from once-feared epidemics; hi-tech hospitals save tiny preemies and patients in need of a new kidney or heart. But we are still mortal. And even if we have been successful in warding off plagues that decimated earlier generations, we have no lack of our own – from suicide, abortion, divorce, and addiction, to racism, poverty, violence, and militarism. We live, as Pope John Paul II has said, in a culture of death.

It is also a culture of fear. Fearing old age, we hide our elderly in nursing homes. Fearing crime, we protect ourselves with guns and locked doors. Fearing people who don't look like us or earn as much, we move into segregated or "gated" neighborhoods. Fearing other nations, we impose sanctions and drop bombs. We are even afraid of our own offspring, turning our schools into virtual prisons, and our prisons into holding pens and morgues. Add to all these anxieties several more that are driving millions to distraction, at least at the time of this writing: terrorism, bio-warfare, and planes falling out of the sky.

With eight children, and some two dozen grandchildren, I know what it is like to ponder the future and be scared. Having stood at the bedside of dying friends and relatives – and having fought alongside them – I also have an inkling of what it means to face death. More important, I have seen the peace that radiates from those who have not only battled their fears but found strength to overcome them. That peace gives me courage and hope, and in telling you their stories, I hope it will do the same for you.

Ordinary men and women, the people in this book had their share of bad days, struggles, obstacles, and low moments. They cried; they were scared; they needed re-assurance. Most would have gone under without sup-port. But to me their significance lies not so much in the way they died, but in the way they prepared for death, whether aware of it or not: by living life to the full, and not for themselves, but for others. None of them were anywhere near perfect, but in serving a cause greater than themselves, they were given eyes to see beyond their own needs, and courage to bear suffering without being defeated by it.

One person I knew died so suddenly and so recently that I am still coming to terms with it. A Franciscan priest and a fire department chaplain, Father Mychal Judge was going about his daily business in New York City's Church of St. Francis when a fellow friar rushed into his room to tell him that he was needed right away at the scene of a fire. The date was September 11, 2001; the place, the World Trade Center, which had just been hit by two hijacked planes and was engulfed in flames.

Donning his uniform and rushing downtown, Father Mike was soon at the base of the Twin Towers, where he joined hundreds of others — mostly rescue teams — con-verging on the scene. The details of what transpired next are unclear: some say he administered last rites to a dying firefighter; others remember him standing alone in silent prayer. Whatever happened amid all the chaos, it was his final hour. Shortly before Tower One collapsed, his lifeless body was discovered in the lobby and carried to a nearby church.

Aside from his chaplaincy work for the Fire Department of New York, Father Mike was an outspoken advocate for people dying of AIDS; he was also known throughout the city for his love of the downtrodden. With a pocketful of dollar bills "rescued" from friends who could afford to give them away, he always had something to give a needy person on the street.

In 1999 Father Mike and I traveled through Northern Ireland with a mutual friend, NYPD Detective Steven McDonald, promoting dialogue and reconciliation. We made a second trip to Ireland in 2000, and at the time of his death, we were in the final stages of planning a similar one to Israel and the West Bank.

Father Mike spent his last hour on earth encouraging others by turning to God; and that is basically the same reason I put together this book: to encourage you by pointing you toward God. In him, as these stories show, there is comfort and strength for even the most anxious soul.   *Rifton, New York*

1

Foundations

My one-day-old sister Marianne died when I was six. I never even saw her alive, yet she influenced my childhood as few others did. Her birth and death had a decisive impact on my sisters and me, as well as on my own children years later.

It was 1947, and my family lived in the backwoods of Paraguay, in a small Christian commune that ran a primitive hospital. Just before Marianne's birth, after two days of extremely difficult, life-threatening labor, my mother's heart suddenly gave out. Luckily, the staff was able to resuscitate her, but she remained unconscious. My father pleaded with the doctors to perform a cesarean, but he was warned, "Your wife will die if we operate. The only way to save her is to abort the baby; otherwise both mother and baby will be lost."

It was an incredibly difficult situation: both my parents believed firmly in the sanctity of all life. Papa went out into the woods to pray.

When he returned, Mama had regained consciousness, though she remained in critical condition. Then, unexpectedly, the baby was delivered naturally. She had a small bruise on her head from the instruments, but otherwise she seemed healthy. My parents were certain that God had intervened.

Yet Mama sensed that not all was well with her child. Marianne did not cry, nor did she open her eyes. The next day, she died. A few weeks later, Mama wrote to her brother in Germany:

> It is so hard to grasp that this child, whom we longed for so greatly, and who was born in such pain, left us before we got to know what kind of person she would be. Sometimes it all seems so unreal, like a fleeting dream. But the more I think about it, the more grateful I am Marianne was born alive. She brought us great joy, if only for a few hours, and she led us to a deeper love for one another. In this way, despite the brevity of her life, I feel that she fulfilled a task on earth.

As for Papa, he thanked God for the rest of his life that the baby had not been aborted. The experience cemented his belief that no matter how long or short a soul lives on earth, it always has a divine purpose. He passed this belief on to me in the form of a deep reverence not only for the mystery of birth, but also of death, and for the sacredness of every human life, regardless of its span.

At the time, of course, I remained an ordinary youngster, full of mischief and frequently in trouble. Like most of the boys I grew up with, I had a passion for bareback riding and secret hunting excursions, and I loved to watch the gauchos work their herds and race their horses. My imagination ran wild with dreams of being a gaucho one day. Still, Marianne's impact on me was always there, like a seed that slowly germinated and took root in my heart. It is still there.

Life was luxuriant in our subtropical paradise, but disease and death lurked around us as well. We saw glimpses of human misery every day at our mission hospital, where I often went with Papa to deliver food and supplies. Many of the patients suffered from malnutrition. Leprosy and tuberculosis were prevalent. There were complicated maternity cases, children dying of respiratory ailments, meningitis, or dehydration, and men injured by falling trees or wounded by machetes after drunken brawls.

Papa often told us children about Jesus and how he came for the poor. He told us about men and women through the centuries who gave up everything for the sake of Jesus. One of our favorite stories was that of

Vassili Ossipovitch Rachoff, a young Russian aristocrat who left his family and wealth and walked from village to village to help the suffering and dying. I thought about Rachoff long and often.

As a teenager I spent several months away from my family, working at a mission house in Asuncion, the capital of Paraguay. My job consisted mainly of running errands and doing odd jobs around the house.

Often I skipped the Sunday morning service and disappeared into the slums, where I had many friends. Their living conditions were appalling – crowded bamboo shacks with open sewage running between them. The flies and mosquitoes were horrendous. Hundreds of children roamed the alleys, many of them orphans, and expert thieves. Some worked shining shoes – five cents a pair – a job I found so intriguing that I soon got myself a kit and joined them whenever I could. Bit by bit these children told me about their lives. Many of their parents had either been killed in fights or had died of tropical diseases. They had seen siblings die of illnesses or deficiencies, and they themselves had survived only to continue living in hardship, fear, and danger.

When a revolution broke out in the city, much of the fighting took place right on our street. We heard the rumble of nearby tanks and machine-gun fire all night. Bullets whizzed over our house. From our windows we saw soldiers being killed. This was war, and I was thirteen, separated from my family, and scared. What if I were shot?

My great-aunt Monika, who lived in the house with us, noticed how afraid I was and consoled me. A nurse, Monika had served at the front during World War I, and she told me how dying soldiers would lay their heads on her lap and weep like little children in their pain and fear of death; how they cried with remorse for their sins; how they agonized because they would never see their loved ones again. Through her deep faith, Monika had touched them, comforted them, and turned them toward Jesus before they died.

Still, the questions ate at me: Why do people have to die? And why is there so much evil and wickedness in the world? Monika read me the passage from Romans 8 about how all creation groans for redemption. She lessened my fears, especially the fear of death. Like Papa, she told me that somewhere in the universe, Christ is preparing a place for us, and I felt it was a very real place, not something abstract. Many times I was reassured by this belief. I also found comfort in Jesus' wonderful promise in the Gospel of Matthew, "Lo, I am with you always, to the end of the world."

Some ten years later, I again encountered death in a very personal way. (My family was by now living in the

United States, having left South America to help build up a new branch of our commune in Rifton, New York.) The Civil Rights movement was in full swing, and no one could be indifferent to it. Martin Luther King was (and still is) an inspiring figure for me. His belief in the cause of justice was unwavering, and he seemed utterly fearless, though he was hated by so many, and threatened so often, that death must have continually lingered at the back of his mind. Just days before his assassination he admitted as much – and explained why he refused to yield to fear:

> Like anybody, I would like to live a long life. Longevity has its place. But I'm not concerned about that now. I just want to do God's will. And He's allowed me to go up to the mountain. And I've looked over. And I've seen the Promised Land. And I may not get there with you. But I want you to know tonight that we as a people will get to the Promised Land! So I'm happy tonight. I'm not worried about anything. I am not fearing any man. Mine eyes have seen the glory of the coming of the Lord!

To me, King's life carried an important message. In the spring of 1965 a friend and I traveled to Alabama, and experienced firsthand King's deep love and humility. We were visiting the Tuskegee Institute when we heard about the death of Jimmie Lee Jackson, a youngster who had been seriously injured eight days earlier when a peaceful rally in nearby Marion had been broken up by the police.

Bystanders later described a scene of utter chaos: white onlookers smashed cameras and shot out street lights while police officers brutally attacked the black rally-goers, many of whom were praying on the steps of a church. Jimmie, who had seen a state trooper mercilessly beating his mother, had tackled the man, and was shot in the stomach and then clubbed over the head until almost dead. Denied admission at the local hospital, he was taken to Selma, where he was able to tell his story to reporters. He died several days later.

At the news of Jimmie's death, we drove to Selma immediately. The viewing, at Brown Chapel, was open-casket, and although the mortician had done his best to cover his injuries, the worst head wounds could not be hidden: three gashes, each an inch wide and about three inches long.

Deeply shaken, we stayed to attend Jimmie's memorial service. The room was so crowded that the only place we could find to sit was a window sill at the back; outdoors, the grounds were packed as well.

Amazingly, there was not one note of anger or revenge to be heard in the service. Instead, an atmosphere of courage and peace radiated from the congregation. And when everyone rose to sing the old slave song,

"Ain't gonna let nobody turn me 'round," the spirit of triumph was so powerful that an onlooker never would have guessed why we had gathered.

At a second service we attended in Marion, the atmosphere was decidedly more subdued. Lining the veranda of the county court house across the street stood a long row of state troopers, hands on their night sticks, looking straight at us. These were the same men who had attacked Marion's blacks only days before. As we left the service for the burial, we passed first them, and then a crowd of hecklers that had gathered at nearby City Hall. The police, who were armed with binoculars and cameras as well as guns, scanned and photographed each one of us; the hecklers, though unarmed, followed us with insults and jeers.

At the cemetery, King spoke about forgiveness and love. He pleaded with everyone present to pray for the police, to forgive Jimmie's murderer, and to forgive those who were persecuting them. Then we held hands and sang, "We shall overcome."

Though meeting Martin Luther King was a formative experience, no one influenced my outlook on death and dying as much as my parents. Papa suffered a great deal in his lifetime. Several times he was gravely ill, almost to the point of death, but miraculously he always pulled through. Mama, who was four years older, was vigorous, active, and hardly ever sick. We children always assumed that Papa would die long before Mama. But God had other plans. In September 1979 Mama was found to have cancer of the lymph nodes. Her health deteriorated rapidly, and soon she, who had spent her life serving others, was an invalid who needed to be cared for – a fact she found hard to accept. Yet in spite of her great suffering, she trusted in God and submitted to what she felt was his will for her. She found peace of mind and faced the end without fear.

On the day the doctors informed our family of Mama's sickness, my parents wept, and we wept with them. Then they looked at one another – I will never forget the love in their eyes – and turning to us children said, "Now every day, every moment, counts. We must not miss any chance to show our love to our brothers and sisters, to the children, to our guests." Mama told us to trust completely in God's wisdom and leading. It was a heartbreaking but deeply moving moment.

Just months later, in the winter of 1980, three elderly members of our church died within a two-week period. All three had been close to my parents for many years, and their deaths cut deep into Mama's heart. With each one, she became noticeably weaker. First Papa's mother –

my *Oma* – died at the age of ninety-five. It pained Mama that she was not well enough to prepare Oma's body for burial or to set up the room in which she was laid. She had always felt it a privilege to do this "last service of love," as she called it, for members of our community.

When Dora, a woman Mama had known for almost fifty years, passed away only a few days later, I took my parents to see her for the last time. Mama looked at her with unforgettable tenderness, and though she was unable to attend the funeral, she still got out of bed and stood trembling in the doorway in respectful silence as Dora's burial procession passed our house.

The next week Ruth, an old classmate of my father's, died. For her funeral, Mama got dressed and sat up in her bed. It was clearly more than she had strength for, but she insisted on showing her deep love and respect for Ruth.

Children from our church often came to visit Mama, and their confidence that she would recover had an immediate effect: when they were there, she became peaceful and radiated joy. Often she said with a sigh, "The children, the children!" She didn't know it, but they met many times in secret to pray for her recovery.

Mama died in March 1980, five months after her illness was diagnosed. Her death was such a heavy blow for my father that he would never recover from it. Papa and Mama had been married for over forty years, and they had always worked together and depended on each other for advice. Now Papa was alone.

Over the next two years his physical strength declined rapidly. He read his Bible daily and held worship services when he could. He also spoke often about God's ultimate plan for all creation, saying repeatedly, "God's kingdom is all that matters. Each of us is so little, so weak. Yet each of us is also an opening for God's love to break into this world. That is what I want to live for; that is worth dying for." This attitude stayed with my father until the end.

During the last weeks of Papa's life, he could hardly speak, but it was still inwardly strengthening to sit with him – God's nearness was palpable, and it gave him a deep peace. He died early one summer morning, and it was a privilege for me, his only son, to close his eyes forever.

2

Fear

I was born in England in 1940, in a time of fear. German bombers flew nightly right over our home in the Cotswold countryside, heading toward nearby Birmingham, and on their way back they would randomly drop whatever they still carried. Several times bombs fell very near our house, and my mother later told me how she often agonized over the safety of us children.

In 1955, when my family came to the United States, the Blitz was a distant memory, but another war – the Cold War – was in full swing, with both superpowers racing to build the most powerful weapon. The horrors of Hiroshima and Nagasaki were still present, and the nuclear hysteria that had developed since then was at an all-time high. Schools had regular air-raid drills, and families built their own bomb shelters and stocked them with canned goods. Newspapers carried stories about possible Soviet attacks on American cities.

For me, living in the United States was an exciting adventure. At the same time it was frightening to be reminded that Rifton, our new home, was within the ninety-mile radius that experts predicted would be doomed if an atomic bomb were ever dropped on New York City.

I never got used to the drills. Again and again I fought my anxiety of bombs and war, and I sensed a similar anxiety in many of my classmates, despite the jokes. Others of my generation will, no doubt, have similar recollections.

Fear, of course, is not limited to particular places or eras. It is a universal emotion, if not a primal instinct. Each of us has felt it — recoiling from a sudden burst of flame or a snarling dog, for instance, or grasping at a railing and backing away from a sudden drop-off. But there's another type of fear: the fear that comes with serious illness and the prospect of death. This fear has less to do with self-preservation. It is fear of an uncertain future, fear of change, and perhaps most importantly, fear of facing one's life squarely and coming up empty-handed.

When Matt, a 22-year-old I knew, was stricken by a malignant lymphoma a few years ago, we talked about this fear, and those conversations have stayed with me ever since. Like most patients who have just been diagnosed with a serious illness, Matt was primarily concerned with his physical condition, at least at first, and peppered his doctors with all sorts of questions. What was the cause of the lymphoma? How effective was the treatment supposed to be? What were his chances of survival? What did this or that medical term mean? Within a few days, however, his overriding concern had changed to his spiritual state. It was as if he sensed that his life had taken an irreversible turn and that no matter what the outcome, he needed to set it in order. As his family doctor later remembered:

I dropped by Matt's room two days after he'd been discharged and noticed that he'd been crying. I asked him what was up and he told me, in brief, that he had had a long talk with his dad and that he felt he had to deepen his life. He said there were things on his conscience that he needed to tell someone about. He also said he felt "scared and lonely."

I suggested that he try to get out of the house in the next few days, even if he felt rotten. Maybe that would help. But he just looked past me and said, "My relationship with God is not what it should be."

I assured him that all of us needed to deepen our lives, not just him, and that his illness was helping us all to realize our need for God. Matt just lay there with big wet eyes, staring straight ahead, absorbing the gravity of his personal situation. Looking at him, I suddenly realized that each of us needs such a moment.

Around the same time, Matt sent me an e-mail in which he wrote:

> There's a passage in the Letter of James that is very important to me right now. It talks about telling each other your sins so that your prayers will be heard and answered. Making sure that all of my sins are confessed and forgiven, and asking forgiveness of people whom I've hurt, has never been so important to me as it is right now…more important than physical healing. When your need for God outweighs your need to appear flawless in front of the people around you, repentance becomes something you long for, not dread. I experienced this very personally when I came home from the hospital. I knew it was literally a matter of life or death to straighten out my relationship with God if I was going to get through my illness.

In the days that followed Matt sent me numerous such e-mails, and I tried to answer him in return. One thing I told him was that having cancer means having one's personal power dismantled, and that perhaps God was trying to speak to him through it. I also reminded him that he'd had everything going for him up till now: he was young and strong, handsome and gifted. He had the world by the tail. But perhaps God couldn't use him with all his gifts. I said, "Matt, maybe God had to bring you low, so he could work through your weakness. Now you have to ask for strength to accept it." Amazingly, he replied, "I hear you. It's going to be hard, but that's what I have to do."

Matt changed greatly over the following months. At the time he was diagnosed, he was a brash and often loud-mouthed joker; happy-go-lucky on the surface, but privately terrified. Six short months later, however, he was a different person. True, he never lost his silly streak, and was still scared at times, even near the end. But having gone through days and nights of the most excruciating pain, he had developed a new, deeper side. And having stopped looking for an escape from the hard fact that he was dying, he had come to terms with the thought, and faced it head on. In doing so, he found strength to meet the agonies of death calmly.

Not everyone dies peacefully, and it's not just a matter of emotional make-up or personality. Peace cannot be found solely by "working through" one's feelings, as people often put it. There's no question that doing this can help us quell our fears – especially in the sense of allowing ourselves to be vulnerable, like Matt did, and turning to the support of those we trust and love. But fear cannot be conquered by emotional catharsis or will-power. Even a hardened soldier will cry out for his mother at the moment of death.

In my experience, there is a definite correlation between fear and the "hardness" of a soul. For a person who is conscious of his weakness, it is a relief to admit his limits and ask for help. For an independent person who sees such vulnerability as defeat, however, it is terrifying, especially if he has steeled himself against the idea of "giving in" to death for a long time. Suddenly he sees his self-reliance as the illusion it always was, and realizes that even the strongest man is helpless when confronted with his own mortality.

In her recent memoir, *Body Toxic,* author Susanne Antonetta illustrates this vividly. A woman who always had everything under control, Antonetta's grandmother ruled her household with an iron hand and an unyielding opinion on everything from food, clothing, schedules, and careers, to the choice of her children's mates and the prospective names of their babies. (If she didn't approve, she vetoed them.) But when death came, she was gripped by an uncontrollable fear:

> It was terrible to see someone so afraid to die. There were no platitudes – a life well lived, dying surrounded by a healthy family, being remembered – that could encircle the

enormity of her fear. Our presence offered her nothing. We could have been winked out of existence for all she cared. She grew haggard with her fear, her jowls and ribs shrinking, her eyes wild and distracted. She'd lost the charming carelessness of the woman in love with her solitude.

My grandmother died haunted. I don't mean just by her death. She saw ghosts and phantoms every night when she went to bed, hiding in her room and pouring in through the windows. They made her scream. She lived in a world of bad spirits. I'd moved far away by then so I don't have my grandmother's descriptions of them, just my mother's laconic ones: "Oh, you know. Bad."

Antonetta's depiction of dying is not pretty, but it is unusually insightful in drawing the connection between the personal and the cosmic. After all, we are never alone, but are surrounded at all times by the two opposing forces of evil and good. And though the battle between them is played out in many arenas, I believe it is most intense wherever the soul of a dying person hangs in the balance.

Dorie, a close friend of my mother's who felt continually tormented by this conflict, lived with it not only at the end of her life, but for decades. Dorie lived next door to our family for many years, first as a part of my parents' household and, after their deaths, as part of my own.

The Dorie most people knew was a happy person who found great joy in helping others. When a baby was born, she was the first to arrive with fruit, flowers, and an offer to clean the house. It was the same when guests were expected. Nothing satisfied her as much as making sure the extra room was dusted and the bed freshly made. She was endlessly cheerful, it seemed, and willing to do the most mundane chore. She never expected or wanted thanks.

Underneath, however, Dorie was a nervous, anxious person. She had trouble sleeping at night and always wanted to have someone nearby. She worried over every symptom of aging and dreaded the prospect of physical ailments or disabilities. By fifty she was already worrying about dying. Thankfully, her determination to be of use to other people and brighten their day kept her afloat – and prevented the fears that plagued her from driving her to the brink.

Then cancer struck. For six years Dorie battled it bravely. Initially she underwent several rounds of chemotherapy, each of which found her so apprehensive and distraught that she required continual emotional support and pastoral counseling as well. Luckily, she pulled through and went on to enjoy several cancer-free years.

Then came a relapse. This time the cancer grew rapidly, and we knew Dorie did not have long to live. She was in severe pain, and radiation provided only partial relief. Sitting with her and talking seemed to help more. With her, my wife and I sought for answers to her questions: What is death? Why do we have to die? Is there life after death? Together we read many passages from scripture about death and resurrection, searching for verses that would strengthen her. I reminded her that she had served God and those around her for decades, and said I felt sure he would reward her.

All the same, the last weeks of Dorie's life were an enormous struggle, both physically and spiritually. One sensed it was not just a matter of ordinary human anxiety, but a vital fight for her soul and spirit. She seemed besieged by dark powers. My wife and daughters nursed her for days on end and accompanied her through long hours of inner torment. Once she cried out that something evil had entered her room. With what little strength she had, she threw a pillow at it, shouting, "Go away, darkness! Go away!" At such times those of us with her would gather around her bed and turn to God in song or in prayer. Dorie loved the Lord's Prayer very much; it was always an encouragement to her.

One morning, after a particularly restless night, Dorie's fear was suddenly gone, and she said, "I want to depend on God alone." She was full of joy and anticipation of that great moment when God would take her, and felt it would be very soon. She said, "There's a surprise today: the kingdom's coming! When it comes, I will run downstairs and outside to welcome it!" That same afternoon she exclaimed, "All my pain is gone. I feel so much better! Thank you, thank you, God!" A little later she said with a smile, "God will call me home tonight."

In the evening, she called my family – her adoptive family – together and hugged each one of us in farewell. We sang and prayed by her bed, and she remained peaceful through the night. She slipped away from us for good as dawn was breaking.

Having fought as long and hard as she did, Dorie's departure was nothing less than a victory. She knew what it was like to be gripped by cold fear, but she clung to her belief in a God who was greater than her anxieties and never let them completely overwhelm her. And as she breathed her last, she did so with the calmness of those who have come to realize, as the first Christian believers expressed it, that the world is merely a bridge between earthly and eternal life: "Cross over it, but do not build your house on it."

3

Despair

While some people appear to sail through life, others seem to slog wearily from one struggle to the next. We may never know why this is so, but that is no reason to pretend it doesn't happen.

Often we shy away from talking openly with a troubled person, thinking that our concern might be interpreted as interference, or that it might push him or her closer to the edge. In my encounters with suicidal depression, however, I have found the opposite to be true: people afflicted by it usually have a desperate need to speak openly about their thoughts. Tragically, they often don't, because they fear a breezy response along the lines of "Cheer up; you'll soon get over it."

Every situation is unique, and it's impossible to anticipate the best way of responding to a person who is depressed. Ultimately, however, words alone cannot save a person. They must be accompanied by the steady support of a loving relationship whereby we can, as the Apostle Paul put it, "carry each other's burdens, and so fulfill the law of Christ."

In the 1970s my father brought home an alcoholic named Terry. He was thirty-two years old, homeless, and a veteran. As a child he had been sexually abused, and the terrible memories of his childhood often pulled him into deep depression. Papa spent a lot of time with him, listening to him, counseling him, and simply being his friend. He also arranged for him to receive psychiatric help and medication. Everyone loved Terry, and he stayed with us for more than a year.

Then one day Terry left, haunted by the demons of his past. Soon afterward we heard that he had killed himself. The news was a tremendous shock, especially to my father, who had loved Terry dearly. It was as if a family member had died. He wept for Terry, and he wept for the pain of the whole world.

One could almost say that it was futile to try to help a man like Terry; that he didn't have a chance. Yet I have experienced over and over again that there are plenty of people whose wounds *can* be healed and who can be helped to overcome suicidal tendencies.

Over the past decades many desperate people have turned to me for pastoral help. Often their personal lives were in turmoil, and anguish over relationships, jobs, or money matters had upset the delicate balance of their emotions. In other cases there was simply no rational explanation to be found.

For years, suicide has been spoken of only in whispers. Despite our culture's reputation for tolerance, a stigma still adheres to taking one's life. Even as a topic of conversation, it remains largely taboo. People avoid speaking about death, regardless of its cause. When it comes to suicide, they are reluctant to say anything at all. How often have you seen suicide listed in an obituary as the cause of death?

At the same time, according to recent studies, a person commits suicide every fifteen minutes in the United States alone; and children between the ages of ten and fourteen are twice as likely to take their own lives as they were a decade ago.

Clearly, suicide is a devastating, widespread problem. For most of us, it has probably crossed our own minds at some point. Why, then, is it so hard for us to address? Perhaps it is because we are unwilling to see how near the brink of despair we all stand.

I have known Jim since his childhood, so when he fell in love with a woman named Sheila, it was my privilege to offer pastoral guidance as their relationship developed. Later I had the joy of conducting their wedding service.

Married life began happily for them, and within a year their first son arrived in perfect health. Then one morning a few months after the baby's birth, Jim was at work when he began to feel uneasy. It was uncanny, he would explain later, but somehow a voice inside him seemed to be saying, "Sheila is in trouble!" He called her workplace. She wasn't there. Then he called their home. No one answered, so, panicking, he left work and ran the quarter mile to their apartment. Finding a letter on the bed, he ripped it open. Then he looked in the bathroom. There she was, out cold on the floor, a kitchen knife and an empty bottle of extra-strength Motrin beside her...

Later, Jim would look back and recognize the warning signs that had been there all along – signs he had missed, or chosen to ignore. He would remember times Sheila tried to tell him about the dark thoughts that often harried her, and how he'd tried to bring her around by changing the subject. He would come to understand the desperation that had driven Sheila to act. But that morning, as he dropped to the bathroom floor and shook his wife's shoulders, screaming her name into her ear, all he could think was, Why?

The demon of despair lurks at the edge of every human heart, and if we are honest we must admit that each of us has at one time or another felt its chilling touch. Despair is one of our greatest enemies. It means the loss of all joy, all hope, all confidence – sometimes even the will to live. Naturally, as with any illness, we look for a cause in hopes of unearthing clues to possible remedies. Often self-accusation lies at the core of despair. Many people spend their lives in darkness, ruled by a sense of guilt. Sooner or later they are tempted to self-destruction. Sometimes their guilt is real; other times it is merely perceptional – even the most unremarkable weaknesses and vices are exaggerated and turned into seemingly insurmountable walls.

Feelings of worthlessness and inadequacy are another reason for suicide. To be sure, such sentiments are normal. There are times when we feel we are not deserving of love or friendship but, like Kafka's beetle, insects worthy only to be squashed. Many elderly people see euthanasia as a simple solution to their complex problems: loneliness due to the death of spouse or friends, loss of control and independence, and feelings of being unloved. They fear being a burden to their families, experiencing emotional or physical pain, and perhaps most of all, a long, drawn-out dying.

Finally, every person, believing or not, is subject to evil as a very real power. It is the work of the devil, whom the Bible calls "the accuser" and "the murderer from the beginning." Satan knows our weakest points and strikes directly at our souls, using every means, including mental illness, to break us down. He throws people into deep despair and depression, into a dark heaviness that may not lift for years. When we see suicide in this way — as a battle between spiritual powers — it encourages us to let go of our inclination to despair and to turn instead to God's infinite understanding.

Many who attempt suicide do not really want to die. Their desperation is a cry for attention, a cry for help. It must not be ignored, but taken seriously. One unsuccessful attempt is often followed by another. Without help and intervention, it will only be a matter of time before it succeeds.

How can we help such people? Many prevention programs exist, and such initiatives have their place. But I sometimes wonder whether we do not rely too heavily on experts. When a person is desperate, an "expert" may be the last person he wants to face. After all, who can cope with analysis or advice when he feels unable even to face himself? Naturally one cannot rule out the use of medications, but we should not forget that often the simple support of a listening ear — whether of a friend or family member, pastor or priest — is of decisive help.

Suicide stems from sickness of soul — from a soul starved of love. What better prevention than to help children, from infancy on, to find joy and purpose in life, to point them towards God? Perhaps one of the main reasons for our culture's high suicide rate is our forgetfulness with regard to Christ's two greatest commands: "Love God with all your heart, soul, and mind; and love your neighbor as yourself." I am convinced that, taken seriously, these age-old words can still lead us to answering — and overcoming — the deepest despair in the world.

Another antidote we should not underestimate is prayer. However poor and inadequate our prayer may be, it is the best remedy for despair. And even if we think we don't know how to pray, we can turn to God. Praying with the Psalms can be especially helpful, since the psalmist frequently voices our innermost longing in prayer: "Give ear to my words, O Lord, consider my sighing…" or, "In my anguish I cried to the Lord, and he answered by setting me free." Even when we feel attacked by darkness and God seems far away, prayer can be a mainstay.

When we pray it is as though we cling to a rope God has thrown to us. If we hold fast to this rope — no matter how numb the arms of our heart — he can pull us to safety and freedom. As Jesus says in the Gospel of Matthew, "Come to me, all who are heavy laden, and I will give you rest. Take my yoke upon you, and learn from me; for I am gentle and lowly in heart, and you will find rest for your souls." And for those who feel too unworthy to pray, Romans 8 offers this comfort: "The Spirit helps us in our weakness...and intercedes for us with groans that words cannot express."

When such verses fail to comfort a suicidal person, it is up to those of us near to him to have faith and believe in his stead — and, once again, to pray. No matter how certain a person is that he is beyond help, it is still possible to keep him afloat with the reassuring knowledge that others will continue to intercede on his behalf. There is a profound protection in this. As Dostoevsky says, "A prayer for the condemned will reach God, and that's the truth."

But what about when our best attempts at prevention don't work, when someone threatens to kill himself anyway? According to the Hebrew prophet Jeremiah, who says that "a man's life is not his own; it is not for man to direct his steps," we ought to do everything we can to save him. But we must never try to do this by means of harsh or judgmental words. A hurting soul needs compassion, not condemnation; and despite his admonition, Jeremiah himself was tempted by suicidal thoughts, writing, "Cursed be the day that I was born! Oh, that I had died within my mother's womb, that it had been my grave! For my life has been but trouble and sorrow and shame."

There are other passages in scripture, too, that acknowledge the travails of living, and the human tendency to lose hope in dark times. To quote Thomas Merton's paraphrase of verses from Luke and Revelation, "In the time of the end there will no longer be room for the desire to go on living. Men will call upon the mountains to fall upon them, because they wish they did not exist; they will wait for death, and death will elude them."

None of this is to imply that suicide is a good or valid choice for a severely depressed person. Like most believers, I feel that because killing oneself almost always entails rebellion against God, it is wrong. But my point is this: it is not for us to pronounce it an unforgivable sin. Almost everyone struggles with suicidal thoughts at one time or another, and when someone actually tries to follow through on such thoughts, they need understanding, not judgment.

Earlier in this chapter I told of Sheila's attempted suicide. Prompt medical intervention prevented her from dying, and after a two-week stay at a local psychiatric ward where she turned the vital corner — from wanting to kill herself, to wanting to live — she was back at home with Jim. But that was hardly the end of the story. Before long, her old demons returned, and some weeks she found herself battling suicidal temptations almost daily.

For the next several years Sheila's life was an emotional roller coaster — the uphill slopes marked by optimism and confidence that healing was in sight, the downswings eased by medication, pastoral and psychiatric counseling, and intensive prayer.

Sometimes it seemed like a journey through hell, for her condition seemed largely the result of guilt she carried from a promiscuous and desperately unhappy adolescence. Eventually she came to feel that the only way forward was to face that guilt and find redemption from it.

Often Sheila and Jim would come to me for advice. Sometimes I was able to offer it; at other times I wasn't. On those occasions there was nothing to do but sit quietly and plead for God's intervention and help.

Today, seven years after she tried to kill herself, Sheila is the mother of three growing boys and one daughter — and she is no longer suicidal. She is not so naïve as to see this as a "happy ending," for there are still days, even if rare, when she must battle fear and self-doubt. But having come as far as she has, she is convinced that even when she feels sad or alone, God will not abandon her. "Sometimes I just have to trust that I'm in his hands," she says, "even when I don't feel it."

4

Losing a Baby

The birth of a baby is one of the greatest miracles of creation. After months of waiting and hours of painful labor, a new being comes into the world. Since time began, the gift of new life has been celebrated with great joy. As the Gospel of John puts it, "When a woman is in travail, she has sorrow, because her hour has come; but when she is delivered of the child, she no longer remembers the anguish, for joy that a child is born into the world." Yet there is wisdom in the old saying that a woman in labor has one foot in the grave. Even in our day, every birth is attended by some anxiety for the health of both mother and child, and there is always the chance of something going mortally wrong.

Writing about the conflicting emotions that surrounded the birth of her first child, Dorli, the wife of
one of my nephews, writes:

> Stephen was born seven weeks premature in a university
> hospital. The miracle of his little kitten cry will always
> stay with me. That was the only time his voice was heard. I
> only caught a glimpse of my son as he was whisked away
> to be examined.
>
> Two hours after his birth I was wheeled down to the
> neonatal ICU to see and touch my firstborn. He was
> tiny, less than three pounds, with a shock of dark hair.
> He was attached to every conceivable monitoring de-
> vice, and the ventilator was breathing for him. I was
> filled with joy and thanks for the miracle of our son, sure
> that he would live. My husband, Eddie, later told me that
> he was not as sure as I about Stephen's future. As a vol-
> unteer in Armenia following the 1988 earthquake there,
> he had seen firsthand the fickleness of life and the suf-
> fering of countless people.
>
> Stephen lived exactly twenty-six hours and two min-
> utes. His prematurity compounded several serious medi-
> cal conditions that could not be corrected. I remember the
> tears that would not stop when a group of doctors brought
> us into consultation six hours before he died and told us
> that they suspected a genetic condition that would mean
> his early death. I held on to Eddie and tried to grasp what
> we had just been told.
>
> Our family doctor came to stand by us in those difficult
> hours. It was obvious to everyone that Stephen was dying.

Hard is not an appropriate word for that moment, but I knew that if I let go, Stephen could be released to a future better than we could have given him here. I took my son into my arms while his soul was delivered to God.

It is not only the death of a living child that has such an impact on a parent. In counseling couples that have experienced the trauma of a miscarriage, I've come to realize what a deep hurt and sense of loss this leaves, especially in the mother. Alice, a neighbor who lost a son, says:

> We have had seven children. With our fifth, Gabriel, we never reached the moment of joy that accompanied the safe arrival of each of our others. Just less than halfway through my pregnancy, we found that his chances of survival were very slim. How we longed for this dear child, and at the same time how we knew we needed somehow to let go of him. I was not ready for that. This kind of thing only happened to other people. How could it be happening to us? We saw him several times on the ultrasound, lively and all there, it seemed – *our* baby, and a real little somebody. How could he be taken from us? And then one day his heart no longer beat. Another check, and still no heartbeat. Our little one had died. He was no longer to be.

After the birth, Alice and her husband were able to farewell their son. That was an unforgettable sight, to see her hold Gabriel's beautiful little form, then wrap him tenderly and put him in the coffin, lovingly made by a friend. We then accompanied the parents to the cemetery and sadly buried the baby. Reflecting on the experience, Alice later wrote:

> I think it is important to allow and even encourage parents to meet their grief head on. If this does not happen, it will take years to find healing, or perhaps healing will never take place. Don't be surprised if it takes time to find peace; you have to be ready to really hurt. The grief will always be with you, but you need to reach the peace.

The death of an infant is not only a painful event, but a particularly hard test of our faith. We wonder, "Why did God create the child at all, if it was to live so briefly?" My mother, who lost two children, said she never found an answer to that question. But she did find comfort in her faith that God does not make mistakes, and that because every life bears the stamp of its Creator, even the shortest one carries a message from the world beyond.

Clearly, death is a mystery that no one can satisfactorily explain. But that does not mean we should avoid it. Our culture shies away from death, especially when a body has been mangled in an accident or has been autopsied. Many in the medical and religious field suggest having a closed casket so that family members are saved from facing the cruelest aspects of their loss. But such advice can backfire. After all, death *is* final, and no pains taken to soften its impact can change this. Jane, a woman who, unlike Alice, never saw her baby, writes:

> Our only baby girl was stillborn; we buried her on her father's birthday the next day. The saddest part in it all was that we never saw her or had a chance to hold her in our arms. She was born by C-section after a long, hard, labor. I was very ill, and my husband was all alone. The doctor asked him if they could send our baby to a medical center for an autopsy, to which he agreed. It had been a normal pregnancy, so we wanted to know why our baby died just before birth. However, they never could determine the cause of her death, and we never saw her after she came back. The doctor recommended that we not see her, since her small body was all cut up and falling apart. I myself was in critical condition in the ICU for two weeks. As a result I never had a chance to see or hold our little one.
>
> Although it's been twenty-two years, my husband and I still can't talk about our loss. Both of us carry it with an aching heart. We could tear our hair out that we allowed this to be done to our little girl. We realize now that this was the craziest thing we ever did.

From such experiences I have learned how important it is for parents of stillborn babies to be allowed to acknowledge that their baby *did* live and does have an eternal soul, no less than a baby who was safely delivered. In either case, to have the confidence that God created these small souls for a purpose can provide reassurance even as parents grope to find meaning in the brevity of their child's existence. Giving the child a name can also have an important healing effect, as can talking about the baby with the other children, taking photos or measuring height and weight, or keeping footprints – things to remember the child by in future years, and to know that his life was not just a dream.

Leo Tolstoy, the great Russian novelist, wrote the following after the death of one of his own children:

> How often have I asked myself, and many ask themselves, "Why do children die?" And I never found an answer. But just recently, when I wasn't thinking about children at all any more…I became convinced that the only task in the life of each individual consists in strengthening love in himself, and in doing that, transmitting it to others and strengthening love in them also.
>
> Our child lived so that those of us who were around him would be inspired by the same love; so that in leaving us and going home to God, who is Love itself, we are drawn all the closer to each other. My wife and I were never so close to each other as now, and we never before felt in ourselves such a need for love, nor such an aversion to any discord or any evil.

Still, pain over the loss of a child won't automatically bring parents together. In fact, it may severely test their relationship. Dorli remembers:

> The hardest time was after the funeral. I would go up, often alone, to Stephen's grave and cry and cry.
>
> People are quick to rush in with platitudes. One is the belief that suffering and grief will bring a couple closer together. This should never be assumed. It can be the case, but a child's death can also bring great stress to a marriage. It did to ours.
>
> I couldn't figure out how Eddie could go back to work, stoically (I thought), never shedding a tear. I, the volatile one, wept buckets for months. It was our church and community rallying around us in prayer and practical support – as well as the time factor – that eventually helped me to accept the fact that Eddie was grieving in his own way.
>
> I don't know that our marriage would have survived without this gentle counsel, at times unspoken. It is a work in progress. I still often surprise Eddie with an unexpected rash of weeping.
>
> The death of a child cannot be "fixed." I have come to accept this grief as part of me. I hoped for closure with each of our children that followed Stephen, but though the pain is duller, it will stay until we are reunited.

Each time a baby or small child dies, we are reminded that the earth is not yet fully our home and that our life here is short – like a flower, like grass, like a butterfly.

No matter how young the child, no matter how many hours or days or months we were given to love and know that child, the pain seems unendurable; the wounds never quite seem to heal. What else can we do but trust, with the grieving parents, that in Jesus healing *will* be given, even though slowly, almost imperceptibly.

In a newborn we see innocence and perfection, and we look for the day when the whole universe will be redeemed and all creation made perfect again, the day when there will be no more death. We believe – the Bible assures us of it – that this will happen when Christ comes again. Writer George Macdonald, who lost children of his own, once wrote:

> If the very hairs of our head are all numbered, and He said so who knew, our children do not drop haphazard into this world, neither are they kept in it by any care or any power of medicine; all goes by heavenliest will and loveliest ordinance. Some of us will have to be ashamed of our outcry for our dead.
>
> Beloved, even for your dear faces we can wait awhile, seeing it is His Father, your Father, our Father, to whom you have gone. Our day will come, and your joy and ours, and all shall be well.

5

Reverence

After Ruby gave birth to her second child, Ann, she spent the night, as she put it, in "unshadowed joy." There was every reason to celebrate: it had been a normal pregnancy, the baby was healthy and beautiful, and David, her first child, now had a sibling to grow up with. Two days later, Ann died. As her father, Doug, remembers it:

> When Ann was a day old, the doctor told us that he was very concerned about her, and that already at delivery he had noticed something wrong. Why he said nothing right away we'll never know. In any case, we had to take Ann to a hospital halfway across the state (we were living in rural North Carolina at the time), and since the birth had not taken place at that hospital, Ruby was not allowed to stay with her. We had no choice but to return home. Waiting

for news was agonizing. The hours seemed endless, but we could do nothing. We had no direct contact with the hospital.

On the second day, our precious little daughter breathed her last. Ruby was inconsolable and wept and wept. It only made things worse when the doctors told us the problem – we were Rh incompatible – and implied that there was little hope, medically speaking, for us to have any more children.

Leaving Ruby, I drove out alone to bring Ann back home to be buried. On arrival at the hospital, however, I was informed that her body had been turned over to a local undertaker, as required by state law.

I drove to the funeral home, and was at first received with great courtesy and solicitude. When the undertaker realized I was not there to buy a casket or arrange a funeral, however, he became icy and left the room. I waited at the front desk with the baby's bassinet. When the undertaker returned, he was holding our little girl upside down, by the feet, with one hand. I reached for the quilt Ruby had made for the baby, but before I could do more, the man dropped her into the bassinet. He was cold, disgusted.

On the long, lonely drive home, I had to fight very hard to find forgiveness in my heart. I prepared a grave on our homestead, and together we laid our little girl to rest with very sore hearts.

Extreme as Doug and Ruby's story may seem, it illustrates an attitude that is rampant in today's world. Call it jadedness, indifference, or callousness – it all stems from the same lack of respect for life (and the loss of life), and it shows itself in numerous ways. It is there in hospital settings where "professionalism" demands that patients be referred to by room numbers rather than names. It is there at funeral homes, which often promote lavish spending by implying that to save money is to scrimp and thus dishonor the dead. (Who wants to be known as the family who bought their mother a budget casket?) It is also there where children quarrel – even if behind the scenes – over wills and inheritances, and deny a dying parent the possibility of a truly peaceful end.

Irreverence is also there when, because of our superficiality, we are unable to share someone else's pain or grief, and thus try to gloss it over with forced cheerfulness. Linda, the mother of the young man I mentioned in a previous chapter, says such attempts tend to only worsen an already difficult situation:

> Not long after it had become clear that medically speaking, there was nothing more to be done for Matt, a well-meaning neighbor cheerfully told my husband that she *knew* our son was going to pull through: "Matt's *not* going to die. I just know he's not going to die." Obviously we wanted to believe the same thing. But to hold out a false hope to Matt when it was clear he was rapidly going downhill? That wouldn't have been fair. A few days later a

friend stopped by and told Matt he was "still praying for a miracle." Matt replied, "Thanks, but I think it's past that stage. The main thing now is that I find peace."

During Matt's last weeks, Linda also found herself struggling with what she felt was a general lack of respect for the finality of death — and not only in her son's friends, but even in him:

> Three days before he died, someone brought a handful of rental movies for him to watch, and when I voiced my worry that he might fritter away his last hours on earth entertaining himself, I found myself embroiled in a family fight.
>
> People had brought him videos throughout his illness, and though I knew they meant well, I was always a little uncomfortable with it. It wasn't a question of the movies — though some of the stuff he watched wasn't all that great. I just felt he was using them too often, as an easy out, a means of escape from reality. I didn't think it was healthy.
>
> To be honest, I felt the same about a lot of other things people brought him: beer, hard liquor, dozens of CDs, posters, headphones, a radio, a new stereo system with six speakers, a Rio player for downloading music from the Internet, and on and on.
>
> I remember talking about it with my husband and wondering: Is this really the best way of showing kindness to someone with cancer — dumping a lot of junk on him? Sure, we knew it would comfort him in a material way. But

ultimately, these gifts were just *things* – things to divert him from real life-and-death issues he needed to face. Matt felt the same way about most of it, and at one point he cleared a lot of that stuff out of his room.

Anyway, I was concerned that Matt would want to spend what turned out to be one of the last afternoons of his life watching movies, and I said so. But he did not agree with me at all. He said, "I just want to be able to laugh and forget about things for a few hours! How can you be my moral compass now?" He was so mad.

I was in tears, because I was thinking, "Here's this poor kid who just wants to escape for a few hours. Doesn't he have a right to do that – to have a little fun?" Besides, I had just read this book on death and dying where the author talks about how important it is to create peace around a dying person. The book said, "no family quarrels," and here we were arguing. It just tore me apart.

I love to watch movies myself. But I also felt, and still feel, that it's too easy to escape (or let your children escape) so you don't have to deal with things that are hard. I'm not just talking about cancer. Whenever you are in a struggle – any struggle – you need to set your sights on the things that will strengthen you, not distract you, if you're going to make it through.

On the other hand, I thought, "Matt's upset because I am being too moralistic. I have to listen to him. Maybe he's saying something I really need to take to heart... After all, he's dying! But he's still my son, and I know that escaping is not good for him. Can I risk *not* saying something that might be vitally important for him?" It was one of the hardest moments I have ever faced.

Later, Matt calmed down and said he knew where I was coming from. He said that deep down he also felt that watching movies was a waste of time when he had so little left, and that he actually wanted to spend it with other people. He even thanked me for not giving in.

This is not to say that reverence demands a long face. Far from it. After Carole, a colleague, was stricken with breast cancer, it was her wacky humor as much as anything else that kept her afloat. At one point she even asked everyone she knew to send her their favorite jokes, and as they arrived in the mail, she collected them in a binder "for when I'm depressed and need a good laugh." In Carole's case, it would have been irreverent *not* to share in her goofiness. Shortly before she died, she told me:

I'll be honest: when the time comes (as they say) I hope no one starts singing those hymns about floating around in heaven. I'd think I was already descending into my grave. You know, the words of those songs may be deep, but for some reason, hearing them sung reminds me of all the most depressing things in life. I know it shouldn't be that way, but it is...I need energy, strength for the fight.

It scares the heck out of me to think of everybody standing around and looking all morbid or something. I don't know; I guess every death is different. I hope there's a good basketball game on the court outside my window when I go, and some hefty music coming up from downstairs...

What, then, is reverence? To explain it as the dictionary does — "honor" or "deference" — is a good start, but these words are still abstract. As far as I'm concerned, reverence needs to be experienced to be understood.

I opened this chapter with Ann, a baby who died as a result of her parents' Rh incompatibility. Years later, after new research gave Doug and Ruby new hope, they attempted to have another child. But again things went wrong, and the baby was stillborn. This time, however, their pain was leavened by (in Doug's words) "the redeeming effect of reverence." Given his and Ruby's high hopes, their loss was no less painful. But now, instead of loneliness and a coolly distant undertaker, there was the love of friends, the sympathy of an entire congregation, and the understanding of a pastor who reassured them that "no life, and no hope in the direction of life, is in vain." This support buoyed them so steadily, Doug says, that when they arrived at the cemetery to bury Frances — by moonlight, and carrying lanterns — he did not dread the task before him, but felt like he was "walking into a haven of light."

The Childlike Spirit

As adults, we often seek answers to life's riddles by trying to analyze events and causes. Sometimes this works; more often it doesn't. In matters of illness and death especially, it seems that there is always an element of mystery – something that leaves us in need of more than our own explanations. This is not true of children, however, who tend to possess a greater tolerance for mystery. Even if they tend to fret over what we adults might see as "little things," they are generally far more accepting of life as it unfolds, and are not so bogged down by doubts, questions, and worries over the future. They are also more matter-of-fact about the things that adults fuss over, exaggerate, or over-interpret.

Cassie Bernall, a Colorado teen whose death made headlines after the infamous Columbine High School massacre of April 1999, is a case in point. Confronted by two armed classmates in her high school library with the question, "Do you believe in God?" she bravely answered, "Yes," and was immediately shot. Within days, the international press was proclaiming her a latter-day martyr, and symbol of courage and conviction. Meanwhile those closest to her, while they never belittled her bravery, maintained that she was really an average teen, with ordinary problems and imperfections and weaknesses. As a classmate told Cassie's mother afterward:

> People can call Cassie a martyr, but they're off track if they think she was this righteous, holy person, and that all she did was read her Bible. Because she wasn't like that. She was just as real as anybody else. With all the publicity she's getting – the stories, the T-shirts, the web sites, the buttons, the pins – I think she'd be flipping out. She's probably up there in heaven rolling her eyes at it all and going oh-my-gosh, because she'd want to tell everyone who admires her so much that she wasn't really so different from anybody else.

There's another reason Cassie might roll her eyes – her childlike faith, which would have surely left her baffled in the face of all the fuss over the meaning of her "martyrdom." As her mother, Misty, recalls:

One day, a week or so before Cassie's death, we were sitting at the kitchen table, talking, and got onto the subject of death. I don't remember how. She said, "Mom, I'm not afraid to die, because I'd be in heaven." I told her I couldn't imagine her dying – that I couldn't bear the thought of living without her. She replied, "But Mom, you'd know I was in a better place. Wouldn't you be happy for me?"

In retrospect, Cassie's frank statements about the afterlife seem uncanny. At the same time, they have reassured Misty as she continues to grapple with the loss of her only daughter: "But Mom, you'd know I was in a better place."

Mary, another mother who lost a child, found similar comfort in the thought that her son Pete was in God's hands. Pete, a five-year-old, died in a totally different setting – New York City, in the summer of 1960 – but his departure was no less sudden.

A happy, tow-headed little boy with blue eyes, Pete loved to play in the sandbox in front of his house with his cars and trucks. When his kindergarten class set off for the Bronx Zoo one August morning, Pete was high with excitement. He wore his new sneakers and best shirt. Little did anyone dream that it would be the last day of his life.

About three in the afternoon, his mother took a call from Mt. Sinai Hospital: Pete had been admitted for what was presumed to be heat stroke. Mary was frantic: her husband, Wendell, was on business in Europe, thousands of miles away, and she herself was two hours from the hospital. Driven by a neighbor, she left immediately for the city. On arriving at the front desk of the hospital, she was informed that her son had been put on the critical list. Why? How? What on earth had happened? She called my father, her pastor. Stunned, he spread the word throughout our congregation, and everyone who could gathered to rally for the little boy by praying for him.

Pete remained comatose, however, and his condition worsened. Nonplussed, the doctors did everything they could think of; an off-duty specialist even came in to see if there was anything she could do. But it was all in vain. At about ten in the evening, the end came. No one could believe it. Just that morning Pete had left home so full of life. Now he was gone, and his father, though on the way home, hadn't even arrived yet.

Only the next day did the picture unfold: while the children were watching a mother monkey with its baby, the teachers had noticed that Pete — with them only moments before — was missing. Beside themselves with worry, they had alerted zoo officials immediately and searched every imaginable place. Finally he was found, curled up, unconscious, on the back seat of the school van in the parking lot. How had he found his way among the cages, the crowds, the maze of city parking lots, to the van? And who else, if not his guardian angel, could have led him there?

On the day after Pete's death, our neighborhood stood silent in a state of disbelief. Not only Mary and Wendell, but every parent and teacher in the community, was cut to the heart by the sudden turn of events. Not so the children, however. They were much more matter-of-fact. The day before, they had been watching the animals at the zoo; now they were discussing all the things Pete would see in his new home, heaven, and painted a large picture of an angel carrying him there amid stars, galaxies, clouds, and rainbows. They also remembered the songs Pete had liked, and sang them over and over.

Four decades later, Mary says that though time has numbed her pain, how and why Pete died is still a mystery to her. But that has not prevented her from accepting what happened. Like Pete's classmates, she has found peace by trusting in God: "I've learned to accept God's will, even if I can't comprehend it. A lifetime is too short to take in all that God wants to say when he calls a child to himself. Yet I believe he's always saying something through it."

Several years ago another family I know lost a child – this time to cancer. Unlike Pete's death, Mark John's was not sudden; yet it, too, shows how the childlike spirit can overcome the morbid gloom we so often associate with dying, and turn it into a redemptive experience. To quote from his parents' diary:

> The doctors at Yale-New Haven proposed that Mark John, who was then three, be transferred to a hospital in New York City for rigorous chemotherapy along with some other new treatment still at the experimental stage. When we asked them how much it would help Mark John, they could only say that at best it might prolong his life two to eight months, and at the price of his becoming deathly sick. When pressed, they reluctantly admitted that he would suffer terribly; in fact, he could die from the treatment itself…
>
> We decided that we would rather have our child at home, close to us, than in a hospital, even if he would live a little longer. It was an agonizing decision, but we knew that God alone has all our lives in his hand, and especially the life of our little boy.
>
> Daily Mark John became weaker and weaker. After a few weeks our pastor suggested that we bring him to a service where we could lay him into the arms of the church and intercede for him. We knew Jesus could heal him, but we also knew that he might want to have him back…

The service was very simple. Our pastor spoke about how Jesus loves all the children of the world, and then we prayed that God's will would be done, and that we would be ready to accept it.

Easter had special meaning for us, thinking of Jesus' suffering and deepest pain, his godforsakenness and need for help, and then the resurrection and its unbelievable promise to every believer. Mark John was surely a believer. He believed like Jesus told us to – like a child.

On Easter morning we took him on a long walk in his wagon, and his mother talked to him about heaven and the angels and Jesus. She told him he would soon go to heaven, and that he should wait for us, and someday we would all be together again. He listened and nodded and sometimes said, "Yes." Later, when the rest of the family joined them, he pulled his big sister down to him and whispered joyfully, "Natalie, soon I'll get wings!"

Then Mark John lost his sight in one eye. He cried when he realized it. We were in such a tension: Would he be blind before Jesus came to take him? We longed so much that he might be spared that ordeal.

Once when he was lying on our bed between us, he asked us about the picture hanging on the wall opposite our bed – a painting of the Good Shepherd leaning over a cliff to rescue a lamb, with a bird of prey hovering over it. We knew a bird of prey was hovering over our little child too, but he was so unaware, so trusting. He grew thoughtful as he looked at the picture and asked us to tell him about it. We told him that Jesus was the Good Shepherd, and that we all are his lambs – also he. It was remarkable how he listened intently and seemed to understand...

By now he was eating hardly anything at all. He got thinner and thinner, and we feared he would starve. We wondered how long our other children could endure to see him suffer so much, as this illness slowly but terribly distorted and changed his dear face and body. Yet somehow, love showed us the way. All the children wanted to be with him. They accepted his suffering completely...

One day when we bent over him as he lay in his little wagon, he reached out his thin arms and cried pitifully, "I can't see, I can't see!" We said, "When you are in heaven – when your guardian angel comes and carries you to the arms of Jesus – you will be able to see again." But he could not be comforted. He asked, "When? When?" and we said, "Soon." He argued and said "No," so I had to insist, "I promise." Then he grew calm.

A day or two later, when we said goodnight to Mark John, he reached up and said, "I want to kiss you, Mommy," and gave her a healthy kiss. He kissed his mother first and then me. We were both so moved and happy because he hadn't asked for a kiss like that for several days: his little head turned towards his Mommy with his precious eyes that couldn't see any longer...

Often during the last days we talked with Mark John and told him that he was a brave boy, that we were very, very happy that he had come to us, and that he always was a good boy. On two occasions he answered us very emphatically, shaking his little head and saying, "No, no." It distressed us. We didn't know what he meant, but in retrospect we feel that maybe he just wanted to remind us that he was also sometimes naughty, and that he was sorry for it.

On the last day he vomited blood; our doctor turned to us and said, "Soon." Then we sang a song that we had sung many times during the last days: "We shall walk through the valley of the shadow of death." When we came to the refrain, "Jesus himself shall be our leader," Mark John said distinctly, "Yes, yes, yes."

Mark John was given incredible strength in his last hours. Several times he said, "Up, up!" We asked him if he wanted to go up to heaven, and he said, "Yes." At one point we said, "Good-bye, Mark John," and he said, "Not yet." That was about an hour before he was taken.

A little later, as we were bending over him, he suddenly said, "Laugh!"

"What, Mark John?"

"Laugh!"

"But why should we laugh, darling?"

"Because," was the short but emphatic answer. And then, while we were still trying to grasp it, he repeated, *"Please,* laugh!"

Then we said, "Good-bye, Mark John," and he said, "Bye-bye." We told him we would see him again soon, because for him in eternity it will be very soon. Then he lifted both his arms and stretched them up and pointed with both fingers toward heaven, and his eyes looked and saw – his blind eyes that couldn't see any longer on this earth, but already saw beyond our world – and called out, "Not two! One!" He repeated this two or three times. "Not two! One!" He saw two angels coming to fetch him, and we had always told him only about one.

Then he turned toward his mother and said distinctly and tenderly, "Mommy, Mommy." Then he said "Papa, Papa." It was as if he wanted to unite us very closely. And then, in that dear and characteristic way of his, nodding his head, he said, "Mark John, Mark John." It was as if he had heard Jesus calling his name, and was repeating it. We had never heard him say his own name like that before. We bent over him, and then two more times he lifted up his arms and pointed to heaven with those thin arms that had been too weak even to lift a cup to his mouth for days.

Then, fighting for breath, he called out, "Mommy, Mommy, Mommy, Mommy." Ellen talked to him softly and reassuringly…He was still breathing heavily but we could not feel his little heart any more. And then came the last precious breath and the agonizing sigh. Death had taken his body, but his soul was victorious and free. We called to our darling little boy, "Mark John, Mark John!" But he was gone. Our doctor said, "It is all over now. His soul is free and with God. He has no more pain." We asked, "Are you really sure?" He replied, "I am sure beyond doubt." It was between three and four in the morning…

As we look back on that night, we can see now that Mark John was slowly moving into another world. He went trustingly, even happily. It was as if we were standing before the gates to eternity, and we could take him that far, but then we would have to leave him. He would go in, and we would have to wait.

7

—

Anticipation

Though death is the last thing most of us have on our minds on a normal day, there are times when circumstances force it to the forefront of our thoughts. A bad accident we pass on the highway; a terrorist attack, natural catastrophe, or violent crime reported in the news; the diagnosis of someone we know or love with a serious illness such as cancer – all these things remind us how death strikes at random. Suddenly dying is no longer a distant prospect – something for other people to worry about – but something we have no choice but to confront. Whether we do so fearfully or with confidence makes all the difference.

I have met people who say they'd rather die a quick death than undergo the drawn-out suffering of a slow one. Still, in three decades of counseling I've never met a dying person who wasn't grateful for the chance to prepare for death.

When Winifred, an elderly editor I know, was scheduled for heart surgery, she looked forward to the possibility of a new, healthy lease on life. She had suffered for years from a debilitating condition, and her doctors recommended heart valve replacement. On the other hand, she did not ignore the seriousness of the procedure, and privately prepared for the worst.

She started with her desk. Though it normally was strewn with messy piles of books and folders on every available surface, the afternoon before her surgery it was uncharacteristically bare: everything was stacked neatly, as if waiting to be sorted by someone else. Later the same day she asked a co-worker, Kathy, for a chance to talk privately. Kathy says it was "nothing big" – a few misgivings that still burdened her conscience after many years, including an incident when, as a teacher, she had been overly harsh and impatient with the children in her care.

Winifred came out of surgery in a semi-conscious state, and died several days later – without being able to say goodbye to her husband and their five daughters. Winifred was seventy-nine, and had a host of medical complications. Had she *not* had surgery, and died of her heart problems, no one would have been surprised. As it turned out, however, her daughters were beside themselves with grief and self-reproach. Everyone had known there were risks. But this was the last thing they had expected. Hadn't the doctors been confident that everything would go well, and said that their mother would come out of surgery as a new woman? Besides, their father had successfully undergone the same operation not long before.

But even if the family did not anticipate Winifred's death, it was clear from Kathy's conversation with her that she herself had. And through the difficult months of mourning that followed, it was that knowledge, more than anything else, that was a lifeline of comfort and peace.

After 35-year-old Rilla was diagnosed with cancer, she underwent surgery and went into remission. Two years later, however, the disease crept back, and it soon became clear that further medical help would be futile. Believing that there was nothing accidental about the recurrence of the disease, she decided that this time she would not fight it, but accept it as God's will. Rilla, a tall, red-haired woman with a radiant smile, was a person you could not forget. Soft-spoken but not reserved, she loved the beautiful things in life: flowers, music, poetry – and children. At the same time, having come of age in the turbulent years of the late 1960s, she was painfully aware of life's ugly corners, and was always looking for ways to reach out to prison inmates, elderly shut-ins, and the mentally and physically disabled. She continued to do this even after her illness began taking its toll.

Toward the end of her life, after she became too exhausted to go out, Rilla wept for the need of the world, especially for the suffering of children, saying, "Our hearts are so small, but we can still wish that they are somehow stretched wider, to pray for all who suffer."

Rilla's cancer was diagnosed during my father's last days on earth, and she was the first dying person I counseled without my father's advice. Previously I had always depended on his support.

Like many sensitive souls, Rilla could be a torn, rather complicated person. She was easily distressed about her perceived shortcomings, and she struggled for years to find a personal faith. Through sharing in the experience of my father's last days, however, and realizing that her own death was not far off, life suddenly became simple for her.

One day Rilla asked me to baptize her, which I did one week after my father's death. The strength her new-found faith gave her was remarkable. She said, "I am experiencing grace in my life; the richness and fullness of God!"

As her illness progressed, she felt the urgency of using each day to prepare for her final separation from those around her. There was much she wanted to accomplish. One project involved sorting through her poetry collection, which contained several pieces she had written, and deciding who should get each piece. Her brother Justin, who helped her, says she did this in such a carefree, light-hearted manner that it perplexed him. She noticed, and the next morning, saying that she did not want to add to his pain, she apologized for talking to him about her death. But in retrospect, as with Winifred, Rilla's willingness to look the future in the face was a help to those who mourned her. The courage that had emanated from her in life became something for them to hold on to after she was gone.

Lynn was diagnosed with leukemia in 1979, just after her sixth child was born. At first, chemotherapy and radiation put her cancer into remission; then it returned. A second round of treatments, too, slowed the disease and fed hopes for a recovery. But it wasn't to be. Soon her leukemia was flaring a third time.

Specialists urged Lynn to consider experimental treatment, but once she found out that it would mean traveling to a faraway hospital, she decided to forgo the treatment.

Besides, as her husband James later put it, they both felt that God held their family in his hand, and they wanted to entrust the future to him alone.

This didn't mean sitting and waiting for death, however. Sensing how little time she had left, Lynn methodically set about to prepare her children for life without their mother. She saw to getting bigger beds for them and extending their quilts to fit; she made them each a photo album and special baby outfits to keep for their own future families. In consideration of whoever might care for them after she was gone, she put their clothing and belongings in order. Beyond that, she lavished time and attention on friends and neighbors, and prepared herself inwardly to leave this life and enter the next. As Lynn's pastor commented, she was like one of the five wise virgins mentioned in the Bible. She had filled her lamp with oil, and was prepared to meet the Bridegroom.

As her strength waned, Lynn was less and less able to spend time in the family living room; whenever she did, however, she was there fully, listening to the children tell of the day's activities, settling a quarrel, or reading a story. Even when nausea confined her to bed, she did not relinquish her role as mother, but took as much time as possible with each child. At the end she could only reach out with her eyes. Lynn died at home, in her own bed, surrounded by her family.

Not everyone is given time to prepare for death. All the same I know of several people who – though they had no obvious foreknowledge – must have had some sense that their time on earth was limited. This was true of Rachel, a nine-year-old who lived in the Paraguayan village where I grew up.

While making toffee over an open fire, the common means of cooking, Rachel's mother was called away "only for a moment." Just then Rachel bent over to stir the candy, and her dress caught fire. She screamed and ran for help, her other clothes bursting into flame. Her father heard her cries and came running, rolled her on the ground, and quickly extinguished the flames. But the damage was done: one-fourth of her body was severely burned.

Brought directly to a nearby mission hospital, Rachel was given the best possible care, but over the next days her condition worsened and she suffered terribly. Her doctors used a short-wave radio to consult with a specialist in Asuncion, the nearest city, but his advice was futile: fluid loss depleted her strength, and by evening of the fourth day she was unresponsive.

By now it was clear that nothing more could be done to save Rachel. Her family gathered around her bed, singing the songs they knew she loved. At one point her mother spoke to her, and she unexpectedly sat up and sang a few lines with them. During the next hours she remained conscious, even holding a few brief conversations with her mother, and singing to herself. Early the next morning she had a relapse, however, and passed away.

Several days later her family remembered that some time before the accident, Rachel had given away most of her few belongings. Then, just the week before, while sitting outdoors with her mother and watching the stars, she had brought up the subject of death and asked about God. No one could be sure, of course, but in retrospect it seemed that she was intuitively preparing for her own departure.

8

Readiness

Xaverie, an energetic, cheerful woman, was a devoted wife and mother. Her illness came in the prime of life — she was thirty-three — and it struck suddenly, just after the birth of her second child, Gareth. First her eyes ached, then she had stomach pains, then lumps on her scalp. She began by taking Tylenol; within a week she was on morphine. Several days later she was gone.

When Xaverie found out she had cancer, she was almost awed by it. To her husband, John, she said, "Well, God does not ask us to carry more than we can bear, so he must feel that I can carry this." And to her mother: "You know, my greatest fear in life was that I would get cancer. Yet the minute I heard I had it, I had absolutely no fear." Later her mother, Sibyl, wrote, "When we heard her diagnosis, she said, 'John, Mama, I want no long faces, no tears. I don't want this to be a big holy experience. I want it to be a joyful, childlike one.' I gulped inwardly, and possibly John did too. How in the world were we going to put on this brave face?"

Xaverie saw her illness as a call to give up her love of life and her family for the greater love of God, and her years of daily surrender to Christ gave her strength to make this new, greater sacrifice. Naturally she loved her children dearly, but she felt she now had another task — to ready herself for dying — and she did not cling to them emotionally. When arrangements were made for a neighbor to take over their care — something most mothers would have found difficult — she accepted the help gratefully, and thanked the woman from her heart.

Incredibly, she never once expressed any anxiety about the future, and from the time she became ill until her death, no one heard her breathe a word of complaint or saw her shed a tear.

One day when my wife and I came to see her, she asked for the laying on of hands, a blessing described in James 5, which reads, "Are any among you sick? They should call for the elders of the church and have them pray over them, anointing them with oil in the name of the Lord."

A few days later, in answer to this request, we held a service for Xaverie. The gathering was quietly hopeful, but it was also heartrending. Everyone present was shaken, and there were many tears. We all felt the presence of eternity in our midst.

Xaverie arrived on a gurney, with an IV-line and oxygen, and as she entered the room, she waved cheerfully and tried to sit up. In a photo that captured this moment, you can see the anguish on John's face. But hers is shining with expectancy and joy. As I laid my hands on her, she looked at me trustingly and said, "With God, everything is possible!" But while she was certain that she could be healed if that was God's plan, she was also completely ready to die.

The next morning my wife and I visited her again and said, "Xaverie, we trust in God's will for you. Are you ready for eternity?" She assured me that nothing burdened her conscience, and that she was at peace: "I will accept God's will, whatever it is. I am ready." In the evening of the same day she died.

It is nothing less than a grace when a terminally ill person is able to set things right and find peace with God — when there is time to beg forgiveness and to forgive, to overcome estrangement and heal old wounds. But time is not granted to everyone.

Rick, an accomplished carpenter, had always suffered from asthma, and there were times when it was so severe that his doctor feared for his life. Nevertheless, he was a cheerful, outgoing person who enjoyed a good joke and loved children.

Then one day he died from a hemorrhage of the brain, leaving his wife, Liz, and eight children between the ages of one and fourteen. There was nothing unusual about the way the day had begun. After getting up early to see his eldest daughter off to high school, he had eaten breakfast with the rest of the family, and left for his job at a nearby factory. Liz was surprised when he showed up at the door sometime later, apologizing for not having helped her get the children up that morning. But there was no indication that anything was wrong.

Toward the end of the morning, however, Jeff, a co-worker, found Rick leaning against a stack of lumber complaining of a severe headache. It was not like Rick to take breaks at work, so Jeff knew it must be serious. Helping him to lie down, he sent someone else running for a stretcher. Minutes later, Rick was not responding. He was rushed to the hospital, but was beyond help. He died the same evening, snatched in the prime of life. Everyone was stunned.

Ephesians 4 advises us to make peace every day "before the sun sets." Rick did this, and the same day the sun went down forever on his life. It has always been a source of comfort to his wife that there was peace between them when he died.

Fred, an engineer, died even more suddenly. Supervising work at a construction site one morning, he began to have chest pains. An electrocardiogram taken at a nearby doctor's office showed signs of a heart attack, and an ambulance was called. Fred's wife, Margaret, was called and arrived quickly, but soon left again to pack for a hospital stay. Moments later, Fred, who was still lying on the examination table, complained of dizziness and then lost consciousness. Desperate attempts were made to save him, but they were of no avail. Advanced cardiac support was not yet developed, and defibrillators were not standard office equipment. When Margaret returned, less than an hour later, she was met by the unbelievable news that her husband was no longer alive.

Back at the construction site, news of Fred's death spread quickly. Work stopped, and before long, flowers were laid where he had been busy only hours before. But there was little conversation. Fred had been a man of few words, and now that he was gone, what better way to pay him respect than to stand in silence?

When death strikes as unexpectedly as it did for Rick and Fred, numb shock is usually the first reaction. Understandably, fear is not far behind. As German writer Christoph Blumhardt once noted, most of us are so consumed by the mundane obligations of the day that almost anything can frighten us, simply by catching us off guard. And to go about life this way is nothing less than dangerous, for it is, as he says, "to go about unprotected, unaware, distracted, and removed from reality."

What, then, does it mean to be ready for death at any time? Can we stand before our Maker to give an account of our lives? Life simply is fragile, and any of us could be snuffed out at any time. In the Gospel of Mark, Jesus exhorts us to watch day and night, "for no one knows the hour of his death," and in his Parable of the Ten Virgins, he warns us what will happen if the "Bridegroom" returns and finds us indifferent and unprepared. But should that frighten us into going around with long faces, expecting the worst?

Martin Luther once said that if the world were to end tomorrow, he would still plant his tree today. A deeply religious man, Luther was no superficial proponent of the old saying "Eat, drink, and be merry, for tomorrow we die." But if his feet were firmly on the ground, his eyes and heart were set on heaven, and this gave him a confidence and conviction that no calamity could shake.

And insofar as we live in a similar awareness of the eternal — and the security of knowing that we are always in God's hands — the same can hold true for us too. No matter what the future holds, it will find us at peace, because our underlying attitude is one of readiness for anything.

When Aaron and Katie and their seven teenage children finally left Ohio for war-ravaged Honduras, their impatience was as great as their exuberance. Volunteers in a 1994 disaster-relief effort sponsored by their Mennonite church, their bus had long been packed with equipment and supplies, and they would have been on the road already, if reports of violence in Central America hadn't thwarted their plans. Now they were finally heading south.

Traveling in a convoy of relief vehicles, they crossed one state after another, and then Mexico, without incident. But one morning several weeks into their trip, as their bus descended a winding mountain road near Tegucigalpa, calamity struck. Daughter Shirley remembers:

I was drowsing when suddenly Dad began to pump the brakes hard and fast, and Mom and Mandy asked him worriedly, "Are the brakes giving out?" I sat up instantly, fully awake. Dad did not answer right away. Then, in an anguished voice, he said they were, and grabbed the CB. My brothers were driving the vehicle behind us, and he told them what was happening. "Pray!" he begged them. "Pray hard!"

We were picking up speed now and heading for a curve. On one side was a huge rock wall, and on the other, a cliff. We yelled at Dad to try steering into the wall, though we knew it could be fatal. But Dad couldn't bring himself to stop the bus that way.

We raced faster and faster, and suddenly we were bearing down on a group of men loading stone into a truck parked on our side of the road. Dad realized he would hit it and began to shake uncontrollably, then tried to swerve around it and lost control of the wheel. "We're heading for eternity!" he cried out; at the same time, I felt the wheels lifting off the ground. Boulders rushed up toward us, and glass rained down everywhere. Then I couldn't see anything…

Sliding down the steep hillside from the highway a few minutes later, Shirley's brothers found her and her sisters badly injured, but alive. Miraculously – considering the crumpled frame of the bus – they had even managed to extricate themselves from the wreckage. Seeing her brothers huddled not far away, Shirley dragged herself toward them. They were trying to console their dying mother:

Mom was gasping hard, and her expression was agonized and helpless. I told her, "Mom, we love you." She seemed to focus and looked straight at me for a second, but then went blank again. That's when I saw Dad lying twisted and lifeless only a few feet away. My heart sank: Dad had always been so strong and comforting – always there for us.

Looking back at her mother, Shirley struggled to "allow her to go," as she later put it.

I was deeply torn. Part of me wanted to cry out, "Mom, live! Please live!" But another part of me wished she could be released from her agony immediately. And so I told her it was all right to go, and promised her that we would meet again someday. Then I turned and tried to comfort my sister Mary, who was lying nearby and seemed near death. When I looked back at Mom, I saw that she had just passed away. I knelt beside her for a long time, numbed by grief.

Aside from Aaron and Katie, everyone on the bus survived, but the next days were still a nightmare. Housed in a government hospital in Tegucigalpa, Shirley and her sisters underwent one battery of tests and surgeries after another. Medications provided relief from pain, but nothing could erase the images that still kept them awake at night: they seemed seared onto their brains. Nothing, that is, except the unexpected peace that washed over her as she viewed her parents before their bodies were flown back to the United States for burial. To Shirley, it was clear: they had both been ready to go.

When I looked into Dad's casket, a deep peace flooded my soul. I saw heaven on his face. He had the most contented look I had ever seen. And when I looked at Mom, I saw the same expression. They looked so happy. There was no doubt in my mind that they were both in heaven.

9

Accidents

Ten years have passed, and still people look at Hillary's son and ask, "Isn't he the one that choked?"

We were sitting in church, in the middle of a service, when an usher called us out. Our son Jarius, who was in daycare, was choking. We got there in minutes, taking three other people we knew from the congregation — two of them medics, and one a nurse. Immediately they began trying to open his airway. Once in a while they got it partially opened, and he would cry out, weakly. In between he was silent. But even then his whole body fought with the medical team as they alternately pounded on his back and suctioned his throat.

Jarius was nine months old — a happy, healthy baby just beginning to explore the world around him. His favorite means of locomotion was rolling sideways, and he could get anywhere he wanted in this fashion. He would roll over to grab a toy, and then lie on his back studying it – or examining his fingers and the way they moved. That morning, he was playing on the floor when his daycare teacher noticed he was having trouble breathing. Luckily, she called for help right away…

As the three rescuers continued to struggle, it was clear that they weren't succeeding. Now he was completely obstructed most of the time, and when he did catch a breath, it was obvious that he wasn't getting enough oxygen. An ambulance was called, and when it arrived my husband, Travis, and I jumped in with Jarius.

On the way to the hospital the team continued to pound and suction; they also monitored his vital signs closely. Unfortunately, we still had no idea what was causing the obstruction. Food? An allergic reaction? Would his airway close off completely before we got to the ER?

Sitting in the front of the vehicle, I couldn't see my son, but I could hear his weak, half-strangled cries, the long, frightening silences that came in between when he was unable to make a sound, and the concerned voices of the medics as they tried to decide what to do next. I felt helpless to do anything but cry out to God inside and pray silently for His protection.

We arrived at the hospital, and the struggle to save Jarius continued. Travis and I were taken aside for history and other questions, and the rescue team went on, pounding and suctioning. They were just preparing to take Jarius to be X-rayed when someone shouted, "It's out! It popped out!" We ran over. There was our son, crying loudly and indignantly — and in the nurse's hand, a small piece of hardware from an adjustable bookshelf, a metal clip my son had discovered and investigated in the best way he knew how: by putting it in his mouth.

We called our church to share the good news, and were told that the service was just over. But that was not all: it had ended with a prayer for our son. And ever since that day, I knew what a power there is in prayer; for I strongly felt — and still feel — that it was the force that released him from his struggle with death.

Not everyone is so lucky. After Evelyn moved in with her uncle and aunt on their Canadian farm, it wasn't long before she was not only taking care of their own children, but half the neighborhood as well. A gentle, fun-loving teen who never seemed nervous, she had a way with children that made them flock to her, and whenever she wasn't working or helping around the house, she could be found playing with her cousins and their friends.

Often they'd be down at the river that ran along one side of the farm. Evelyn and her tag-alongs were forbidden to get wet: the current was strong and there were shifting sinkholes. But summer 1982 was a roaster, and even if you couldn't swim, playing in the cool sand provided at least some relief from the heat. So did wading.

Not one to break her word, Evelyn wouldn't join in at first. But one day she got tired of being splashed and teased, and within minutes she was leading a game of tag in the shallows. Before long, one of her playmates spotted a sandbar a little way out and suggested that they play tag there. Evelyn, the tallest in the group, helped the shorter ones, and they all made it over safely.

When it was time to return home for lunch, Evelyn started back the same way – or so she thought – with a smaller girl holding tightly to each hand. Halfway across the stream, all three stepped into a deep sinkhole. The rest of the children, still on the sandbar, shrieked in terror as they watched the girls struggle to stay afloat. Luckily an older boy nearby heard their cries and came running, dove in, and swam to the rescue. But as all three lunged toward him, he was overwhelmed, and gasped, "Someone has to let go – I won't make it!" Evelyn released her grip, and he began to make for safety with the two younger children.

Once at the shore, he rushed back into the water for Evelyn. But it was too late. She had vanished. By then, more help had arrived on the scene, including Evelyn's parents, who stood in stunned silence and disbelief.

Evelyn's body was later found several hundred yards downstream, caught by a tree. Amazingly, her expression reflected no terror at all. Despite the panic she must have felt as she made her last gasping efforts to stay alive, her face radiated peace.

Accidents do happen. Some are preventable, or seem to be, at least in hindsight. Others are not. In the case of an "unnecessary" death, we may find it as good as impossible to forgive the person whom we hold responsible. It is the same when we blame ourselves, or are made to feel we bear a guilt. But even when we cannot see the way forward, we can always hang on to the heart's deepest longing for peace. And we can pray that it will crowd out other emotions – especially the temptation to grow bitter, or to wallow in self-reproach. In short, we must trust that even if nothing can remove the pain of a tragedy, it can just as soon drive us into the arms of God, as into the pit of despair. That can happen, as long as we are open to such a possibility – as the following anecdote about Karen, an acquaintance, shows.

A missionary in Haiti, Karen lost her three-month-old, Hannah, to a freak accident in their home:

> One afternoon, while waiting for my husband to come home from work, I heated water on the stove to give my daughter a bath. While I got the tub ready and collected a diaper, towels, and pins, she fell asleep on our bed, so I

decided to let her rest for a while. I set the tub down on the floor, tucked a folded towel under her side to keep her from rolling off the bed, and went into the kitchen.

That simple decision changed my life irreversibly. While I was away, Hannah woke up, wiggled to the edge of the bed, and rolled into the tub. I found her just a few minutes later, but it was too late: my baby had drowned. There will never be words to tell you how I felt at that moment. From the depth of my soul I cried to God...

Knowing from other similar incidents how parents who have lost a child in such an accident are often unable to cope with feelings of guilt – and may obsess over the event for the rest of their lives – I asked Karen whether she has ever been able to come to terms with what happened. Naturally, she has done her share of blaming herself, but her overriding state of mind is one of remarkable freedom and peace:

It is nine years ago that Hannah drowned, and I still find myself wondering, "How old would she be now?" "If this had never happened, what would life be like?" And there are still times when I cry in deep sadness. But I would be a basket case if I allowed myself to fill my mind with such thoughts. I have found peace in focusing on my faith that the Creator of all is my shepherd, and that I must follow like a sheep, even if I don't understand the "big picture."

I cannot explain the comfort I felt and feel now in God. It is a mystery. But maybe this quote from Amy Carmichael –

something someone gave me after Hannah's death – touches on the reasons I feel as I do: "We see hardly one inch of the narrow lane of time. To our God, eternity lies open as a meadow. It must seem strange to the heavenly people, who have reached the beautiful End, that you and I should ever question what Love allows to be..."

While one would wish that everyone who seeks healing could find it, as Karen did, it remains a rare gift. And even when it is given, it will not come right away, but only with time. After all, the most pressing question in the wake of an accident (whether fatal or not) is not how to get over it, but to find out how and why it happened. And until we have come to terms with that, "moving on" seems a moot point.

Because accidents always seem senseless, most of us will readily jump to embrace the first plausible explanation that comes our way. And it will come. There's always somebody with a solution, a perfect preventative measure, or an "obvious" lesson on the tip of their tongue. But discovering the deeper meaning of an accident – if it even exists – is much harder. Perhaps that's why Dan, a forty-year-old who survived a deadly fall, feels that in the aftermath of an accident, it is less important to find answers for it than to contemplate the questions it raises:

I was going to Cornell at the time, and one night a bunch of us were walking home from a rock concert on campus. We'd taken a familiar shortcut, but we were stoned and only vaguely aware of just how close it ran along the edge of a deep gorge.

Friends tell me that I was there one second and gone the next. They were certain I was dead. Some of them made their way down to the roaring falls below and searched among the rocks for my body. One went to call the police, and another remained on the path where I'd disappeared. I myself remember nothing at all, except that when I woke up I was lying on my back looking up at a sky full of stars. I yelled for help twice, and the second time I was answered by a voice about twenty feet above me. It was one of my friends, and he raced off to get help. Soon he was back with a student who was a mountain climber. Together they lowered a rope and hauled me back up to the path.

My friends were ecstatic. Someone lit a joint, and we took stock of what had happened. I'd stumbled off the cliff and fallen onto a ledge about three feet wide – the only one of its kind along a mile-long stretch of the gorge. Had I fallen anywhere else, I never would have survived. As it was, I had landed flat on my back, on moss, and I didn't have a single scratch or bruise.

Back at the dorms, we partied up a storm. Yet as we laughed I caught a classmate staring at me as if I were some ghost returned from the dead. I guess I felt like one. I had cheated death, but only by inches.

Still, my fall had little, if any, effect on me. Someone else might have been shattered by it, or awakened to the preciousness of life. But I didn't let myself be fazed in the least. Instead, I partied with fresh abandon.

Looking back, I see now that by mocking the incident in this way, I avoided its impact and missed a rare opportunity to examine my life – its meaning, its direction, its purpose. Yet the fact is that my worldview at the time was such that I was incapable of absorbing any deeper message from it. It was only many years later – after a conversion, actually – that I was able to really think about what had happened and to appreciate its gravity. The protection I experienced that night awes me.

I've had other close calls too, including a near-fatal car accident, and not long ago my mother said something that made me think about them in a new way. She asked, "Where would you be without the pain that brought Jesus into your life?" I've pondered that one often. There is a mystery about the way a death (or a brush with death) can lead us to life; about the way God reaches out and leads us from life's hells toward heaven. We may never grasp it, and probably aren't meant to, but it still happens...

10

Beyond Medicine

I have been doing some thinking about my future. I just saw my doctor on Tuesday morning, and my tumor is not responding to the stronger medication I'm on. I had a big operation and then a round of treatments that was aimed at curing me. It did not work. Now the illness has recurred. Further treatment could prolong life, but it cannot cure the disease.

The more I think about it, the more I feel like opting for no further treatment. It is a most unpleasant experience, and everything in me balks at the idea of going through it again. Also, I can't quite face losing my hair a second time. It is a small point, I know, but a needy one.

In other words, I would like to just live one day at a time. I know if I hold on to Jesus, he will walk through this valley of shadows with me. After all, he's been there himself! I truly believe the words of Job, "I know that my

Redeemer liveth…and though worms destroy this body, yet in my flesh shall I see God."

I know there will be very difficult times, but I want to turn more to my Heavenly Physician and trust in him through whatever lies ahead. He knows best how to heal. He has given me a very full life, and I'm content to give it over to him now.

Bronwen

When Bronwen, forty-nine, wrote this letter to my wife, lumps were reappearing all over her body, and she knew that nothing more could be done. After years of battling cancer, she was (in her words) "finished" with chemotherapy, and tired of waiting for the next test, the next scan. It wasn't that she was tired of living. She was just ready to move beyond medicine.

To anyone who knew how long Bronwen had fought up till then, her attitude was easy to understand. She wasn't giving up – just acknowledging that her struggle had now shifted to a different plane. And she did this so matter-of-factly that no one was tempted to second-guess her. As she wrote in another letter a few days later, "I have a sense of peace about what lies ahead. You do what you can for as long as you can, but in the end, all that is left is prayer."

Sadly, we live in a culture where a decision like Bronwen's is widely frowned on. Polls show that (at least in the United States), the vast majority of terminally ill people would prefer to die at home, as she did – in her own bed, surrounded by the love of family and friends. But the truth is that most spend their final days in hospitals, attached to tubes and monitors, and cared for by virtual strangers. And the result is that instead of being able to use their last days looking over their lives – sharing memories, farewelling friends, celebrating the past (or making peace with it) – they spend them in a clinical setting, fending off the inevitable.

The reasons for this are numerous. On the one hand, the remarkable advances made by medical science in the last few decades alone have raised expectations on every front, and among oncologists and other specialists in particular, the desire to demonstrate invincibility is often extremely strong. As an Ivy League medical professor wrote in a recent article in *TIME*, the "fighter-pilot mentality of success in the face of mortal danger" that is drilled into young doctors leaves far too many of them forgetful of their humanity. "They worship at the shrine of scientific objectivity, and they wrap themselves in a mantle of depersonalization...all in the name of victory over death." No wonder so many find it hard to let go when a dying person insists on relinquishing further treatment – they have been educated never to concede defeat.

But that's only one half of the story. The other is those of us whose unrealistic expectations — for just one more surgery, one more experimental protocol — keep the dying from saying what's really on their mind: "Get me out of this hospital. I want to die at home."

Fear sometimes plays a role, too, on both sides. A hospital, wary of malpractice suits, may prefer to lose a "client" in the midst of a last-ditch effort than let him go home, only to find themselves fighting off grieving relatives who claim the doctor should have done more. And a family — even if they feel they have done everything they could — may still stall at bringing a loved one home to die, because they fear being seen as unwilling to go the extra mile.

As anyone who has ever been involved in end-of-life care will attest, no one set of guidelines could possibly work for everyone. Each human being — even one with exactly the same diagnosis as another — approaches death in his or her own way, and each terminal illness raises its own questions. But it is vital that those questions be honestly and openly addressed.

Sometimes I wonder, for instance, how long the body should be kept alive when it is clear that the soul longs to be released. When the prolonging of life means weeks or months of hospitalization with minimal contact and negligible improvement, we need to be ready to ask ourselves: Are we keeping someone alive for *his* sake, or for the sake of others who don't want to let him go? Are we trying to uphold an ethical standard, or letting ourselves be pressured into something by someone whose main interest is research?

Moving beyond medicine does not mean belittling its role, or shunning the very real assistance it provides in battling infection or relieving pain. But it does mean taking our focus off injections, pills, and white counts, and training it on the social and spiritual dimensions of dying – things that are ultimately far more important.

When it became clear that Pat, an elderly colleague with a long history of heart disease, didn't have much time left, he and his family decided against hospitalization. Doing this meant going against the advice of several specialists – hospitals always seem to have "just one more thing you could try" up their sleeve. And they'll rarely, if ever, encourage you to take matters into your own hands. But Pat's family did, and didn't regret it, even when he died a few weeks later: "We could all be right there, including the youngest grandchildren. It would have been a waste of precious time for him to spend those last days away from home, in some hospital."

Tina, a woman who died at home, made little use of
the medical help she had access to, especially toward the
end. It wasn't a matter of principles: in the last stages of
breast cancer, she was heavily dependent on painkillers
and accepted palliative care. But she insisted that dying
was a family matter, and did what she could to prevent it
from being medicalized. As a nurse recalls:

> Once it was clear to Tina that she was really going to die,
> she made a concerted effort to stay clear of everything but
> the basics. She wasn't rude about it, but she was adamant:
> "If I'm going to die anyway, there's no point in coming to
> the doctor's office, or having blood drawn, or being
> weighed, or anything like that. The important thing is that
> I'm comfortable enough to live."
>
> Refusing to stay in bed, even when nauseated and
> weak, she dragged herself to work (a desk job near her
> house) as often as she could. "I'm not dying of cancer,"
> she said. "I'm *living* with it."

Near the end Tina dismissed her home-care nurses, saying her family could care for her as well as anyone else.
And they did – right to her last breath. I don't believe
there was one nurse or doctor present when she went.

Moving beyond medicine does not always mean moving toward death. In fact, I have even seen the opposite to
be true, as with Hardy, an uncle whose last years remind

me of an old truth: only when man gives up and lays aside his arms can God step in and take up the fight.

My father's eldest brother, Hardy suffered from heart disease and diabetes for many years. In September 1984 he underwent cardiac bypass surgery; in November of the same year his heart failed. Hospitalized, he asked to be released and cared for at home. In early December his blood pressure was dangerously low. At times he was restless or distressed; at other times very peaceful. During moments like these, one felt the closeness of eternity in his room. Once he said, quite simply, "You know, I am dying."

Hardy needed intravenous medications to maintain his blood pressure, and oxygen to relieve his breathing difficulties and chest pain. One day, however, he surprised everyone by trying to pull out the IV. He was ready to die, he said, though just as ready to live. He was ready for whatever God had in mind for him. We called his doctor and discussed the situation at length, then hesitantly agreed to have the IV discontinued. We believed that without the medication, Hardy would not live much longer, and he knew this. It would be a step of faith, but we were ready for anything. Most important, Hardy was.

As his nurse removed the IV, Hardy motioned him to bend over, and gave him a kiss. Miraculously, Hardy survived the next days, gaining new strength daily. Over the next weeks and months he improved even further, resuming his formerly active schedule and even making several long journeys, including one to Europe. Three years later, his heart failed and he died.

It was just as his mother, my grandmother Emmy Arnold, had once written: "Sometimes before death there is a flaring up of life, so much so that one's hopes for recovery revive. It is like a bright autumn before a long, cold winter. And afterward comes spring: resurrection."

11

In God's Hands

To all appearances a healthy baby, Ray became jaundiced within weeks of his birth, and was soon diagnosed with a rare condition: he had no bile ducts connecting his liver and intestines. Though the problem can sometimes be corrected today, it was virtually untreatable at the time (1967), and all that the doctors at Yale could tell Ray's devastated parents was that he would probably not live for more than a year. So they took him home.

Until he was six months old, Ray developed normally, though he was always a little yellow. Then he began to go downhill. First he stopped gaining, and then he began to lose weight. His belly became distended, his face pinched. As his father later said, he looked like a starving child – skin and bones, and big, wide eyes. But his siblings never noticed that, or even took in the fact that he was deathly ill; they just loved him and took care of him, and trusted that he would grow.

Ray died at fourteen months, as the doctor had predicted. At the end his skin was a dark orange, and he weighed only eight pounds.

Even today, in the most scientifically advanced country the world has ever seen — in a world of corneal and cardiac transplants, life-prolonging respirators, and powerful drugs, there is no guarantee that medicine can stave off death. That, perhaps, is the one fact of human existence that has remained unchanged since the beginning of time: our lives are in God's hands.

All of us sense this, even if subconsciously — an agnostic or atheist will cry out "Oh my God!" just as often as a believer when gripped by sudden fear, or doubled over in terrible pain. On good days, however, God quickly takes backstage. We're okay; we've got plans; we've got life in control. Until, like Ray's parents, we find out otherwise.

What does it mean to live with an awareness of our dependence on God? For Adela, a young woman I knew who was struck down with Hodgkin's disease, it meant accepting his intervention in her life even when it meant relinquishing her dreams, and refusing to let cancer stop her from looking forward to the future. Adela was diagnosed in the prime of her life, at twenty-five, and was in love at the time. Illness might have altered the picture for another couple, but not for her and Sergei. In fact, far from throwing a wrench in their relationship, it only confirmed what they already felt: that regardless of her health, her life was in God's hands, and that there was no reason to break off their plans to be engaged and married.

I married Sergei and Adela in August 1985, and I will never forget the conviction with which they answered one question I asked them: "Will you bear with your spouse in joy and in sorrow, in health and in sickness, until death parts you?" Never had that question seemed so important and real.

Humanly, the new marriage didn't seem to make sense: it began against the backdrop of a grueling series of chemotherapy treatments, the first of which left Adela in critical condition. For the next three years, she had to undergo almost continual chemotherapy with multiple complications and frequent hospitalizations. Through it all, Sergei remained loyally at her side.

Later her specialists recommended a more intensive protocol, part of which involved a bone marrow transplant. She underwent this, too, but the benefits were short-lived. Finally she decided to decline all further treatment.

An outgoing person from childhood on, Adela never lost her sense of humor. When chemo made her hair fall out, she painted herself, dressed up as a clown and went from ward to ward, trying to cheer up fellow hospital patients. When the impossibility of having children hit home, she resisted self-pity, and suggested to Sergei that they try to adopt a child. As often happens, their attempts were soon snarled by red tape, but that didn't stop them. Sergei even brought home a crib, and Adela prepared a layette. But nothing ever came of it.

In January 1989, after three years of marriage, Adela passed away. Shortly before, she wrote to her husband:

Please, when I die remember that I was no hero, that I couldn't always accept God's will, that I was a sinner, that I failed in service and love to others, that I knew despair, depression, fear and doubt, and other temptations of the devil. Remember, too, that I loved laughter better than tears, that you can die with cancer but you can also live with it and joke about it. Please don't keep things because I made them or wrote them. They are only earthly things and nothing special. Remember rather that God's will has no "why?" – that his way is best, always; that he loves us even when we don't love him, and that in the church you never stand alone; that hope is greater than despair and faith is greater than fear, and that God's power and kingdom one day will be victorious over everything…

She also wrote a poem that Sergei has allowed me to print:

Beloved Sergei
you may find this as hard to read
as I found it hard to write
but I had to write it
even though it may be many years
before you will need it
I may outlive you although
I can't see how I could live without you
only God knows our hour
but if my time comes
God willing please be near
and tell me that it is the end
and ask me if I'm ready to meet my maker
and hold my hand
pray for forgiveness of my sins
and pray for peace for my soul
and I'll pray for comfort for yours
and fight for you and love you
through all eternity.

As a cliché, "live dangerously" evokes rash judgments and risks taken on a whim. But as Sergei and Adela's short marriage shows, that is not all there is to it. There is something deadening about going through life cautiously – testing the water, toeing the line. But there is nothing as exhilarating as living it to the full. It requires rising to challenges that come your way, rather than evading them; sticking out your neck, instead of hiding in the crowd. It means daring to take false steps – and leaps of faith. And the reward, as we have seen, is calmness in the face of death.

To believe that one is in God's hands, and to draw comfort from that belief, is a gift – and not only for the dying, but for those who mourn them after they are gone. But what about those whom death overtakes without such reassurance? And what about those they leave behind, whose grief is compounded by the worry that the one who died was not ready to go? Especially in cases of divorce or separation, parent-child estrangement, and soured friendships, it is not unusual to encounter fear on the part of those who live on. Where did my ex-husband (or mother, father, son, or daughter) go? Is he with God?

Often, this fear is not limited to worries about where the dead have gone. Believers may wonder how they will fare in the last judgment; nonbelievers may fear the unknown. As a counselor and pastor, I know that far more people grapple with these questions than one might think. Naturally, none of us can speak for the dead, and even if we could, it wouldn't change a thing. God works, as the saying goes, in mysterious ways, and none are as incomprehensible as the secrets of death. Still, there is great peace to be found in learning to put those we love in God's hands — which means trusting that he will not forsake them.

When Lisa was found in a lake near her home early one morning in June 1978, many of her neighbors were uncomprehending. Impossible though it seemed, the particulars of her death made it clear: she had taken her life.

At fifty-five, Lisa had been tested more than anyone I know: of her nine children, one had been stillborn and another had died in infancy. A third was afflicted with a rare bone disease. Lisa herself had numerous medical and psychiatric problems, including eczema, schizophrenia, and Parkinson's disease. She had difficulty walking, and at times her hands trembled so violently that she could not feed or dress herself. On top of all this, her husband had left her.

An active member in a close-knit congregation, Lisa was not without friends. Besides that, she had a good doctor, a nurse who made daily house calls, and neighbors who looked out for her. Her adult children, too, did all they could to support her. But it hadn't been enough, and now she was gone, leaving everyone who knew her reeling in self-doubt, guilt, and grief.

Years earlier, Lisa and I had lived in the same locality, and she had worked as a nurse in the hospital where my wife (also a nurse) had trained. Now we lived hundreds of miles away. We had kept in touch with Lisa over the years, and knew she was prone to depression. But we never would have expected this…

Lisa's funeral, like that of any suicide, was a painful one. Still, my father, a longtime friend of her family, encouraged them not to despair as they struggled to make sense of what had happened. Paraphrasing the author Romano Guardini, he reminded them that no matter how deep our wounds, God, who *always* sees and understands, is endlessly merciful:

> To lose one's mother is to suffer a wound to the heart. But God's love is greater. And in light of this death, especially, it is important that we trust in God, for when we do, he will answer every need. He promises us in the Book of Isaiah that "as a mother comforteth her child, so I shall comfort you."

We may not be able to understand everything a person does, for we can see only his outward appearance, but God, who sees the depths of every heart, can. A person may sometimes do something stupid despite his better judgment: try as he might, he cannot do what he wants to do, or find the right words to say what is on his mind. It is even possible to do something intentionally, but not be able to explain one's intent. All one feels is a restless urge, and the more one tries to fathom it, the more repressed one feels, and the deeper the silence becomes. Such a state of mind can give rise to great torment and suffering. But God still sees and hears…

God's seeing is an act of love. It embraces his creatures, and affirms and encourages them. He hates nothing that he has created. God sees with eyes of love, and there is nothing brighter than his eyes, nor is there anything more comforting…To be seen by God does not mean exposure to a merciless gaze. It means being enfolded in the deepest, most caring, most compassionate heart.

I have always hung on to these words — and not only in relation to Lisa. Five years earlier, an estranged uncle died in a mid-air collision over France. Pastors in the same church, Joel and my father worked together for decades. Over time, however, their relationship became increasingly strained and then fell apart when it came to light that Joel, who was married to my father's sister, was sleeping with another woman. Angry at having been exposed, Joel left his family and the church. For a long time afterward, my father wrote to him, begging him to see the damage he had done, and pleading for reconciliation. But Joel only grew more bitter.

In early 1973, my father received what turned out to be Joel's last letter — a hateful message dripping with sarcasm. Not long afterward came the news of his death. Naturally Joel's wife and children were deeply shaken. Where was he now? And how could his soul ever find rest in death, given the way he had lived?

My father was just as distraught, but he cautioned the family not to rush to judgment. Reminding them of the story of the remorseful thief at Golgotha, he encouraged them to remember Jesus' promise, "Today you shall be with me in Paradise." Surely those words hold true for everyone who repents, my father said. And how did they know that Joel had not sought — and found — forgiveness, if only in the last seconds of his life?

The fear that plagued Joel's family is understandable, especially in light of traditional Christian views of hell. Yet it is neither healthy nor constructive. God judges, it is true, but even in the Old Testament he says, "Have I any desire for the death of a wicked man? Would I not rather that he should mend his ways and live?" And in the New Testament we read, "It is not God's will for any soul to be lost, but for all to come to repentance."

No matter what our grounds for worry, I firmly believe that there are always greater grounds for hope — and for trusting (as the First Letter of John puts it) in the love that casts out fear. For, as we read in Romans 8, "Neither death nor life, nor angels nor hell, neither the present nor the future, nor any powers, neither height nor depth, nor anything else in all creation will be able to separate us from the love of God."

12

Suffering

Whenever I think of suffering, Miriam comes to mind. Born with multiple physical handicaps, including the inability to swallow, she had to be fed by dropper for the first few weeks of her life and by feeding tube until she was one year old. But it was "brittle bone disease" that affected her most severely. As a toddler she would sometimes break a bone just by trying to pull her leg out from between the bars of her crib. Later, a bump into a door frame or a simple fall caused by tripping could mean a series of fractures in her arms or legs or both, often followed by hospitalization and surgery, and always accompanied by much pain, not to mention six weeks or more in a cast. By age eight, she had broken her legs sixteen times.

At ten, Miriam was suffering heart failure. As if that weren't enough, the curvature of her spine, which significantly reduced her lung capacity, left her continually short of breath. By the time she entered adolescence, she was wheelchair-bound.

Then came the biggest blow of all, when she was just fourteen: her mother's suicide. Miriam herself died at twenty-eight, by which time she had undergone at least fifteen operations, been hospitalized more than forty times, and suffered hundreds of fractures.

Throughout her short life, Miriam's personality remained largely free of the burdens placed on her by her medical condition. In fact, she reminded one of a sparrow – small, spunky, cheerful. This was true at the end of her life, too: though she struggled for every breath, she was indomitable. When nothing more could be done for her medically, she said, through her oxygen mask, "Well, I think I'm ready. I only have a few more thank-you notes to write."

Can a lifetime of suffering like Miriam's, or a debilitating illness of any length, ever represent God's will? If we claim it cannot, we are faced with a certain tension. After all, the New Testament tells us of people like a man whose blindness was caused "so that God might be glorified," and that it was God's will that Jesus should suffer and die. On the other hand, because the Bible is so full of passages that speak of God's power to heal and save and give life, it seems incomprehensible that sickness and death should still exist at all.

Writer Elisabeth Elliott points out that though we accept these things, at least on a certain level, as part of life, we find them harder to accept when they "strike down a child, an 'innocent' adult, or someone else whose victimhood offends our notions of fairness. And so we rationalize and theologize and try to come up with answers." In my view, this is often a waste of time. Certainly it can be fruitful to explore the meaning of suffering, to grapple with the "big" questions, and to let them deepen us. At the same time, Elliott goes on, there is a price to be paid "every time we satisfy our need to rationalize such things as suffering. Once we think we have unlocked a mystery, we tend to close the books to further study. Unsolved, the problem captivated us with the challenge of discovery; shelved, it loses relevance and meaning."

Referring to the destruction of New York's Twin Towers on September 11, 2001, author Barbara Kingsolver says:

There are so many answers, and none: It is desperately painful to see people die without having done anything to deserve it, and yet this is how lives end nearly always. We get old or we don't, we get cancer, we starve, we are battered, we get on a plane thinking we're going home but

never make it. There are blessings and wonders and hor-
rific bad luck and no guarantees. We like to pretend life is
different from that, more like a game we can actually win
with the right strategy, but it isn't.

Speaking of blessings, perhaps one of the greatest is the
ability to find meaning in what appears to be meaningless suffering. I say "meaningless" because as long as
pain serves an obvious purpose – the pangs of childbirth, the soreness of exercise, or the surgeon's scalpel –
we are content to accept it. But when we cannot see a
rhyme or reason to it, most of us will react like a cat on an
operating table, which (as C. S. Lewis points out) cannot
possibly know the difference between a vet and a vivi-
sector, and will therefore scratch and bite the first just as
vigorously as the second.

It is all the more remarkable, then, to discover someone
like Alexander Solzhenitsyn, who not only submitted
humbly to hardships he could not understand, but also let
them change him. A famous survivor of Siberia's worst
labor camps, Solzhenitsyn struggled for years to make
sense of his imprisonment. If the state of his confinement
was really a matter of fate, and indicated that he was evil,
he reasoned, it should be easy enough to accept it. But then
what about those who received even crueler punishments
than imprisonment, those who were shot or burned at the
stake? Were they some sort of super-evildoers? And yet,

he noted, it is always the innocent who seem to be punished most zealously. What does that say about those who torture them? Why do they prosper, instead of the good?

In agonizing over these questions at length, however, Solzhenitsyn stopped tangling himself up (as he put it) in the riddle of suffering, and began to make peace with the fact that whether or not he understood it, it would still exist. And with this acceptance came a new insight:

> From then on I felt that the solution to suffering is this: that the meaning of earthly existence lies not, as we have grown used to thinking, in prospering, but in the development of the soul. From that point of view our torturers have been punished most horribly of all: they are turning into swine; they are departing downward from humanity. From that point of view punishment is inflicted on those whose development...holds out hope.
>
> Looking back, I saw that for my whole conscious life I had not understood either myself or my strivings. What had seemed for so long to be beneficial now turned out in actuality to be fatal, and I had been striving to go in the opposite direction to that which was truly necessary for me. But just as the waves of the sea knock the inexperienced swimmer off his feet and keep tossing him back onto the shore, so also was I painfully tossed back on dry land by the blows of misfortune. And it was only because of this that I was able to travel the path which I had always really wanted to travel.

It was granted to me to carry away from my prison years on my bent back, which nearly broke beneath its load, this essential experience: how a human being becomes evil and how good. In the intoxication of youthful successes I had felt myself to be infallible, and I was therefore cruel. In the surfeit of power I was a murderer and an oppressor. In my most evil moments I was convinced that I was doing good, and I was well supplied with systematic arguments. It was only when I lay there on rotting prison straw that I sensed within myself the first stirrings of good.

What does suffering mean for someone who is not granted such a recognition – or who could not accept it, even if he were? Chuck, a fellow pastor, says that for his family and circle of friends, the method of choice was gritting one's teeth and pretending it didn't matter:

> I grew up in a typical middle-class home, where the subject of death – like illness, grief, heartache, or other sources of anxiety – was assiduously avoided. It's not that a conscious taboo existed. But "negative" life experiences were rarely, if ever, discussed outside the family. We simply didn't "go there," conversation-wise.
>
> As a working adult, I found the same silence, the same walls carefully constructed around each personal life. When the wife of an engineer at my firm – a kindly man I regarded as a mentor – came down with cancer, he brushed off every expression of sympathy. It seemed as

though he was obeying some unspoken code whereby vulnerability is seen as instability, and pain as weakness. Obviously he couldn't afford to be associated with either. He had to remain strong.

I know Ed loved his wife dearly, but to this day I am amazed at the lengths he went to detach himself from her suffering, at least on the job. One day he told me rather matter-of-factly that his wife's tumor had burst; a few days later he walked into the office and announced that his wife had died that morning. I was incredulous that he had come to work – though it's possible there was no one at home for him to talk to. On the other hand, the way he dealt with losing his spouse was hardly out of sync with the way everything else was dealt with in our workaday world. There was never any lack of camaraderie, but it was only a façade. When the chips were down, you kept a lid on things – no matter how much you were hurting.

For many people, the belief that pain can be overcome by biting your lip and riding out the storm is coupled with the fear that it is the only thing they *can* do, short of letting down their guard and exposing their true feelings. They refuse to do this, because they feel the mask of invincibility provides at least some protection. But far from shielding them against pain, this mask only hurts them: in hiding their pain from others, it forces them to carry it silently and alone.

Others try to deal with suffering by wishing it away, or pretending it isn't there. But as Fran, who lost a son to cancer, points out, this is strenuous (if not impossible) in the long run:

> Suffering cannot be put off forever, and when it comes, there is no way around the pain. Maybe that knowledge only comes with age and experience. But if I ever have to go through it again in my life, I hope I have grasped it. Life is *hard*, and there are some things that hurt – no matter how much you try to smooth them over or make them nicer. You might as well hit suffering head on when it comes your way, because it won't just disappear.

For Fran's husband, who dragged himself through the first months of their son's illness trying to keep a game face, meeting suffering head on entails utmost honesty – and the willingness to open up about one's deepest fears:

> I kept my concerns about our son's situation bottled up because I was concerned that my wife wasn't handling things. The fact that I didn't allow her to fully share her worries with me created a lot of tension. She needed someone to confide in, someone who could identify with her fears. She needed me.
>
> Then came a breakthrough, when I finally stopped keeping a wall up between us. I allowed myself to become vulnerable. I realized that drawing into a shell could rip our marriage apart. We both knew of marriages where the

pain and struggle that should draw husband and wife closer together actually did the opposite. Couples were driven apart by holding their feelings inside, distancing themselves from one another, and speculating about what the other one thought or felt.

A big part of the challenge was simply dealing with our emotions: the same thing that could make us laugh one day would make us totally fall apart the next. But to admit that you're just a plain, ordinary, weak person, and that you aren't coping, and that it's okay — that is a tremendous relief. If you can do that, you no longer feel the need to deny or suppress your emotions, or to worry if they are abnormal or wrong. If you need to cry, cry.

Once we were able to do this, and to see our stress mirrored in each other, we could share it openly together. We held each other and wept for as long as we needed to. And then we could say, "Well, that's enough for now, let's go on."

In our therapized culture it takes no great leap of faith to believe that "sharing one's pain" like this is the best way to deal with it. But given the number of people I know who have not only coped with enormous suffering in their lives, but come through it stronger than before, I have come to feel that maybe we ought to stop approaching pain as something purely negative. If we allow it, pain can be an occasion for redemption — a crucible of sorts that may refine and renew us. In his novel *Crime and Punishment,* Dostoevsky, no stranger to hardship himself, goes even further, and makes this audacious claim: "You don't believe my words now, but you'll come to it yourself...Suffering is a great thing." Because only someone who has suffered has the right to speak this way, such a statement is best applied to ourselves, not recited to others. In any case, it is rare that someone is given the strength to bear their burdens nobly. Most end up weighed down, if not embittered. All the same, there is a ring of truth to Dostoevsky's words, as the next story shows.

Deb grew up in a comfortable home, attended private schools, toured Europe, and vacationed on Martha's Vineyard. After high school, she attended Smith, an exclusive college for women near Boston. But if her childhood was synonymous with privilege, her adult life was not.

At forty-three, Deb, who was by now married with six children, began to experience numbness in her hands and feet. No medical explanation could be found. Not one to complain, she quietly bore the bothersome problem as it slowly worsened. Soon she began to grow weak and unsteady as well. "Mom can't even help me zipper my jacket," her son Tommy told a classmate. Nor was she able to lift a milk carton off the table without great effort, by clasping it with both hands. Still, she bravely insisted on fulfilling her motherly tasks.

Early in 1969 a lump was found in the back of Deb's neck, and she was hospitalized. An emergency operation removed the tumor, but the surgery left her totally paralyzed below the neck. Almost completely helpless, she could communicate only with her eyes.

But where others saw a ruined body as the main outcome of her ordeal, Deb concentrated on the fact that her life had been spared. Adamant that she would learn to become fully functional again, she saw a physical therapist several times a week, and at home she strained daily to re-teach her muscles to do what she wanted them to do. Part of it was her personality – she had always been a fighter – but there was also another incentive for regaining strength and mobility: she was expecting a child.

Six months after her operation, Deb gave birth to a boy. Miraculously, Mark was strong and healthy, despite all his mother had been through in the previous months. Deb, for her part, was too weak to care for him, or even to hold him for any length of time. But she did what little she could: by propping her arms up with pillows, she fed him by tipping his bottle toward him sideways.

When Mark was six weeks old, Deb entered a rehab program to re-learn the daily activities and skills she had taken for granted all her life, but could no longer perform: walking, writing, tying her shoes, buttoning her blouse, combing her hair, cracking an egg. Despite the tremendous efforts she made, her recovery was only partial: walking proved difficult, her hands shook so that her writing scrawled all over the page, and she remained extremely frail.

For the next several years Deb courageously fought her way back toward normalcy, one painful step after the next. Then, almost imperceptibly, she began to lose ground. Surgery was advised, and she underwent two operations, but neither helped in the long run. For the last five years of her life she was confined to a reclining wheelchair, her body so weak that she could not support the weight of her own head and arms.

Even then, however, she refused to give up. Debilitated as she was physically, she remained mentally and spiritually alert. Refusing to play the part of a helpless invalid, she insisted instead on contributing something in return for the nursing care she received, and put in several hours a day – until a week before her death in 1982 – proofreading manuscripts for a local publishing house.

Coming from a large family and a close-knit community, Deb enjoyed a security and comfort that many do not have – especially nowadays, when loneliness, neglect, and poverty make untold numbers of the disabled and elderly feel that they are a burden, and the once un-thinkable idea of a "right to die" has become an attrac-tive, if morbid, dream for thousands of them.

But quite apart from everything that was done for Deb, there was her own attitude: her resilience in the face of infirmity, her awareness of others who didn't have the care she received, and last but not least, her humble acceptance of her dependence on others — which did not come without struggle.

Deb's view of her suffering is summed up in her reply to a well-meaning visitor who told her, near the end of her life, "If you ask Jesus, he can make you well again." "I know," Deb said. "But he has given me something much more wonderful — my family, and the love of brothers and sisters." At her memorial service, her neu-rosurgeon said that of all his thousands of patients, he felt most privileged to care for Deb. He always felt as if he was ministering to Christ, because Christ lived in her so visibly.

13

Faith

Ed was one of a kind — a single man with a southern drawl, a big heart, and an apartment full of canaries. Formerly an executive for a large Georgia trucking company, he began attending my church when he was already in his fifties. Unpretentious and spontaneous, he had the faith of a child. He was quirky and fun-loving, too, often signing notes and letters with "Edwin Glover Buxton, L.B." — the L.B. meaning "lowly brother."

Ed always said exactly what he thought, when he thought it, and spending time with him meant receiving a running commentary on life — sometimes humorous, sometimes serious, sometimes appropriate, sometimes not. He never married and rarely mentioned his family, yet he loved people, and his apartment was always full of teenagers shooting the breeze and listening to country-western songs like "Achy-Breaky Heart," his favorite.

Ed suffered from degenerative heart disease for years, and as he grew older, he grew increasingly aware that he could "go" (as he put it) at any time. Once he told a nurse who had come to visit him that he was looking forward to meeting God: "I mean, it will be awesome and fearsome, but God and I know each other. He knows about my sinful past. And, you know, he also knows I'm sorry for it." But he was far from pious. Greg, one of the teens who used to hang around Ed's apartment, says he even wanted his funeral to be fun, and told him that when they carried his casket to the cemetery, they should bump into a few trees on the way, for good measure.

One day Ed asked me to come to his apartment. When I arrived he told me there were several things weighing on him, and that he wanted to unburden his conscience. He had nothing heavy to reveal, but after I listened to him and assured him of God's forgiveness, he embraced me and said that this was one of the most wonderful moments of his life. "Now I can meet eternity with joy."

Ed passed away peacefully a few days later. This note was in his pocket: "Around 7:30 P.M. I was sitting here, about to have supper, and I felt a tremendous sorrow for having offended God and sinned against him, a feeling greater than I have ever had before. It could be that I am approaching eternity, so I wanted people to know about this. – Ed."

I held Ed's memorial service, and during it several people rose to speak about his impact on their lives. The voices came from all corners, from teens to elderly people. But the testimony was the same: because of Ed's sincerity and his lack of religious words, his faith had touched them like that of few others and was instrumental in helping them find a basis for their own faith.

Merrill could not have been more different from Ed in terms of his background and personality. But he was like Ed in the solace he found in his faith.

A fellow pastor who worked with me for two decades, Merrill brought an extensive knowledge of the Old and New Testaments to his calling; in addition, he conducted two choirs, counseled couples and high school students, taught Sunday school, and served the church in many other ways.

One day in 1986, Merrill (then fifty-seven) began to have severe nausea and vomiting. Within a few days he was diagnosed with pancreatic cancer. Visits to several specialists confirmed his worst fears – that neither surgery, radiation, nor chemotherapy would be of help. Remarkably, this didn't depress him in the least, but only emboldened him. He even reassured his wife and children that his illness and certain death were going to bring them closer – not separate or defeat them.

Merrill stood helpless before his disease, medically speaking. But he had faith, and it was unshakable. He wrote at the time:

> My future is uncertain. The joy is knowing that it is completely in God's hands. All I have to do is thank him. If I have not much longer to live, then that is God's will and it should mean something. My task is to find out what it means; I have no complaints, only thanks! If it is God's pleasure to give me a chance to start over again, that's wonderful. If it is not his pleasure and he has other tasks for me, I accept that. Faith doesn't depend on me having my way; faith depends on God having his way. This must be my highest joy and delight. Otherwise how can I pray, "Thy will be done"?

About a year before Merrill died, friends sent him information on a homeopathic therapy course available in Mexico. Merrill thanked his friends, and told them that he had "no doubts as to the efficacy of the method...But I have nonetheless decided not to pursue the therapy." He then went on to explain that for him, the joy of being dependent on God outweighed the possible benefits of prolonged life: "My decision may seem mad to you, but I am unalterably firm in it. I joyfully place myself at the mercy of God, and praise him for carrying out his will on my body…"

Admirable as it is, such conviction is not granted to everyone. In fact, there are plenty of people for whom the idea of faith as a weapon against illness is incomprehensible, if not foolhardy. As Merrill would have been the first to point out, such a view doesn't alter God's power or rob him of it. But it does present a challenge. What should one do when a dying person has no belief in redemption or in life after death, and sees no reason to prepare to meet God? What about someone who, like the agnostic eighty-year-old father of a friend, says he can't think of anything more tedious than everlasting life, and mutters about the uselessness of the "F-word," as he calls faith?

As I see it, there is little point in discussing such issues. "Religious" questions tend to divide people just as often as they bring them together, and in any case I feel it is far more important to surround a terminally ill person with compassion than to bring him around to your point of view. Beyond that, there is nothing to stop us from interceding for someone else – whether someone who has lost faith, or someone who never had it. Author Bruce Epperly writes:

When our usual sense of independence and omnipotence crumbles, we must allow others to carry our burdens and shoulder our responsibilities. Sometimes we must even depend upon the generosity and commitment of others for our faith in God…In the gospel story of the paralyzed man, we hear nothing about his faith. We do not even hear the exact nature of his ailment, other than the fact that he had to depend on the efforts of others in order to see Jesus. But we do hear of the great faith of his friends as the catalyst of his healing.

My father used to say that if a loved one lacks hope and faith, have hope and faith for him. *Everyone* goes through periods of spiritual dryness at one time or another, even the most "religious" people. They may feel strong in their beliefs today, but that doesn't mean that they won't be tempted and tested tomorrow.

Mother Teresa of Calcutta, whom the Vatican is currently considering for sainthood, made headlines not long ago when it was revealed that she not only had to struggle to hold onto her faith, but sometimes felt completely bereft. In a recently released letter, she wrote, "I am told God lives in me — and yet the reality of darkness and coldness and emptiness is so great that nothing touches my soul." In another letter she confessed, "I can't tell you how dark it is in my soul — how painful, how terrible. I feel like refusing God...I try to raise my thoughts to heaven, but there is such convicting emptiness that those very thoughts return like sharp knives. Love – the word – it brings nothing."

Clearly, faith is not a trust fund that can be drawn on year after year. It is more like an elusive grail that must be sought and re-won again and again. This is especially so during times of illness or death, when uncertainty about the future, separation, loss, and grief bring on unavoidable temptations – and involuntary change.

This should not dishearten or depress us. In my experience, the battle for faith is the battle that gives life meaning, and the more intensely it is fought, the greater its rewards. Without faith, existence becomes a vacuum that is quickly filled by superficiality, conformity, boredom, and even despair. With it comes strength for each new day.

To someone whose view of religion has been colored by conventional church life, this idea – that faith can be a vital life-force, and not just an obligation or a comforting tradition – may seem unlikely. But it is hard to argue with those who have experienced it as such. Malcolm Muggeridge, England's famed agnostic TV commentator, sought faith for most of his life. At one point, while working as a reporter in Africa, he grew so despondent over his failure to find it that one night he swam out into the sea, intending to drown himself. But at the last moment something held him back. Somehow, from somewhere deep inside, a new sense of purpose and a new desire to live welled up. Muggeridge later explained:

> It is precisely when every earthly hope has been explored and found wanting, when every recourse this world offers, moral as well as material, has been drawn on and expended with no effect...when in the gathering darkness every glimmer of light has finally flickered out – it is then that Christ's hand reaches out, sure and firm.

Kathleen, a retired teacher, found similar strength from her faith as she approached death. Wracked by severe chest pains and shortness of breath, she went downhill gradually, over many weeks. Family members wrung their hands, but she remained calm and reminded them that Christ would not place more on her than she could bear. "He has promised us that," she said emphatically.

For us, as for Kathleen, faith can give more than the hope of a better world on the other side of death. It need not be limited to pie in the sky. By transforming our view of the present world, it can lead us from desperation to courage, and from resignation to resolve. But this can happen only if we allow it to. To paraphrase Mennonite author Clarence Bauman, faith is useless if it is only a matter of halfheartedly singing old hymns and "perpetuating the hope of apocalyptic bliss beyond this sinful vale of tears." But if faith impels us to invest more heavily in the fullness of life, he says, it will open the door to new possibilities of joy and triumph here, in this world – the present world that God created and loves, and for whom Jesus lived and died.

I experienced this triumph at the death of my uncle Herman. My father's youngest brother, this tall, gaunt man once dreamed of becoming a doctor, until World War II interrupted his studies, and sent him first to Switzerland, then England, then South America, and finally the United States, working as a farmer, a teacher, and a minister. Through it all he smoked compulsively, and by the time he was fifty he had developed emphysema.

In August 1972, at the age of fifty-seven, Herman was diagnosed with advanced lung cancer. During the next four months, he needed oxygen almost continually. At times his suffering was so intense that he longed to die in his sleep. As he told me one morning after a particularly hard night, "It's hard to be suspended between life and death like this." He spoke often of eternity, and wondered what it would be like. Surprisingly, he was nonetheless lively and spirited most of the time.

Looking back, it seems that in being forced by his cancer to take stock of his life, Herman was able to see the pitfalls of complacency with unusual clarity – and to recapture the enthusiasm he was known for in his younger years. And he did not keep the insights this gave him to himself, but challenged everyone he knew to rediscover their own "first love" for God.

A week or so before Christmas, on a Sunday morning, Herman's nurses woke him and gave him a bath. Afterward his wife, Gertrude, joined him in the sitting room. Suddenly, he removed his oxygen mask, and a radiant look of joy and peace transfixed his face. Sensing that the end was near, Gertrude called the rest of the family, including my father and me. Minutes later Herman stretched out both arms, clasped his wife's hands, and looked at her – a last, long, loving look. Then he was gone.

Remembering that morning, my father later said, "There was something victorious in my brother's face, and I believe it was the joy of accepting God's will and knowing that it was God's hour for him." I myself have never seen anyone face death so confidently.

14

Courage

As a child I was captivated by the story of the early Christian martyr Polycarp, who was burned at the stake some eighteen centuries ago. Part of it was the drama – the bloody Roman arena of gladiators and saints, lions and cheering crowds. But what struck me even more was Polycarp's willingness to die for his convictions. Not that he went meekly to his death – according to witnesses, he was defiant, and even berated the mob that surrounded him at his execution. But he showed no trace of fear:

> Eighty-six years have I served my king and savior, and he has never done me any harm. How could I blaspheme him? You threaten me with a fire that burns for an hour and goes out after a short time, for you do not know the fire of the

coming judgment and of eternal punishment for the god-
less. Why do you wait? Bring on whatever you will.

After he said this, the mob piled brushwood around him
and (though he was already bound with ropes) threatened to nail him to the stake to make sure he wouldn't
escape. Polycarp remained calm, saying: "Let me be. He
who gives me the strength to endure the fire will also
give me the strength to remain at the stake unflinching,
without the help of your nails."

Like Polycarp, countless men and women – and not
only Christians, but Jews, Muslims, and people of other
faiths as well – have paid for their convictions with their
lives. And I believe we have much to learn from them.
Will we meet death with similar courage and conviction – with the confidence that comes from being at
peace with God and ourselves? Or will we shrink from it
in fear, circling around our regrets and mistakes, and
wishing we had the chance to live life over again?

Because martyrdom is basically an historic phenomenon, such questions may not seem urgent today. But
courage is not an old-fashioned virtue. It is a vital weapon.
And we will not come through the arena of death – an
arena each of us will have to enter one day – without it.
That is why I feel that of all the qualities shared by the
people who appear in this book, courage is the most

notable. Courage in suffering; courage in the midst of emptiness and loss; courage to face the future, even when it means certain death. Without it, none of them could have overcome their fears and found peace.

Certainly courage is just as important in the prime of life as at its end. In fact, if we hope to muster it when we need it most – at the hour of death, for instance – we must nurture it from day to day. And if we cannot find it in ourselves, we need only look around us. In my home state of New York, for instance, stories of the selflessness and heroism shown by police officers, firefighters, and other rescue workers are still surfacing, months after the tragedy of September 11, 2001. And there are always "ordinary" people like Ramona, below. Though unconnected to any public event, and previously invisible except to a small circle of family and friends, I found her story inspiring.

Five months pregnant, Ramona was eagerly looking forward to the future. Or at least she had been – until a routine checkup at the doctor's office dashed her hopes and changed her life forever:

It was a Friday, and my husband, Barry, was working, so I had gone to my checkup alone. The doctor finished my sonogram, and asked me to take a chair. Nothing could have prepared me for what he had to say next: my baby had a condition called anencephaly, which basically meant that he had no skull. The top half of his head would be severely indented, and though he should have no problem staying alive in my womb, he would not survive birth for more than about forty-eight hours.

I was in shock. I had had two miscarriages, but they were so early on in pregnancy that there wasn't much more to see than a sac. This was different. I could see this baby on the sonogram as a real, already-developed person.

I wept all the way home. I thought of the Old Testament story of how God had commanded Abraham to sacrifice his son Isaac. Not that I would be killing my child. But I *would* have to let go of him and give him up to God.

It was the hardest thing I had ever had to deal with, and I couldn't stop asking why. God knew I had loved and welcomed each child he had given me. Why was he doing this to me?

As time went on, however, Ramona spent less time trying to find an answer to that question. Even if she'd never understand why she had been subjected to such a burden, she was determined to accept it, and to carry her baby to term. It was, very simply, a matter of "reverence for God's gift of life," she says.

Once she made her decision, Ramona had to defend it. First her doctor reminded her that since the fetus was less than twenty-four weeks old, state laws made abortion a legal option — and gently recommended exercising it. Friends and acquaintances, too — even members of her church, which is Catholic — asked her why she didn't "do something" about it. But she would not be swayed: "I never once thought of abortion as an option. As I explained to my doctor, and to folks who seemed baffled, my baby was still alive, despite his condition, and as long as God willed that he should go on living, I would go on caring for him."

Ramona's attitude may seem matter-of-fact. In reality, however, it took courage to hold to her decision, and endless prayer. When she flagged, it was the baby who helped her up again: "I could feel him moving inside me, and each time I'd feel a kick, I felt he was reminding me to pray." Asked what she was praying for, Ramona says it wasn't only for her own peace of mind. She also hoped her decision might encourage others to question the widespread belief that abortion is the best solution to prenatal deformities — or at very least to respect her belief as a valid one.

This hope was fulfilled, at least on one count: in December, as she was leaving her doctor's office after another appointment, he said to her, "You know, Ramona, I really admire your respect for life."

On February 4, 2001, Ramona gave birth to Isaiah, as she and Barry named the baby:

It was a sudden, sharp, painful labor. Maybe I was subconsciously resistant to it, just knowing that Isaiah was safe as long as he was inside me. I started crying. But I'd had a friend bring me a picture of Jesus on the Cross, and I placed it where I could see it. I looked at it throughout the next several hours and prayed that Jesus would be with me.

When I finally gave birth, a mixture of emotions flooded over me. I felt both great joy and deep sorrow. Isaiah looked very different from a normal baby. Like the doctor had warned me, the whole top of his head was missing, and his eyes were badly swollen from the unprotected passage through the birth canal. Yet he was living, breathing, and kicking. He was even robust-looking.

Not all of Isaiah's siblings could handle seeing him that first day. My younger children were fine – they didn't even seem to notice anything different about their brother – whereas my fifteen-year-old daughter carefully avoided my hospital room, and went off to the cafeteria with a cousin. But despite her uncommunicative exterior, I knew she was going through a lot underneath. So I was not surprised when it all hung out later. After Isaiah had died, she held him and wept, "Mom, I never held him alive."

Given Isaiah's condition, there was little the hospital could offer that Ramona and Barry couldn't. And so they took him out of the intensive care unit and home to the family. He died the same evening:

I had prepared a small bassinet for Isaiah, but he never used it — we never stopped holding him once we got out of the car. Around 7:30 P.M., his brother, who had him in his arms, said, "Mom, I think Isaiah needs changing." I took him and laid him on the couch, and he suddenly stiffened and turned purple. I had been told to expect something like this, but when the moment came I out-and-out panicked. I felt completely helpless. Handing Isaiah to his dad, I looked frantically for the local hospice number, but when I finally got through, they couldn't seem to make out who I was or what I was talking about. I tried the hospital next, and asked for Amy or Sue, Isaiah's nurses. They came as soon as they could, but it was too late; Isaiah had already died by the time they arrived.

It took him about twenty minutes to go. Right before he died he gave about seven deep breaths — like sighs, with pauses between, and then there was nothing. I bent over him and checked for breathing. There was none. I had never seen someone die before, and this was my own child. I can't forget it, ever.

Asked whether she was angry with God after first hearing Isaiah's diagnosis, Ramona seems surprised:

No — I mean yes, though only at first. A nun I know, Sister Katherine, told me that since Jesus is your friend, and friends get mad at each other, you should tell him everything — be it your anger, doubt — whatever. You can't just act as if whatever he sends your way is fine. But then I thought more about it, and said to myself, How dare *you* get mad at *God*. After all, he's the creator of the whole universe. And who am I?

Ramona says that far from regretting her decision to have Isaiah, she feels it was a privilege. And several co-incidences make her feel that perhaps she was fulfilling a divine obligation as well. First, the day she found out about Isaiah's condition was a Friday – the day Catholics remember Mary, the "Mother of Sorrow." Ramona felt that this was a sign. Second, her own birthday, which is January 22, is designated "Pro-Life Day" on the church calendar. "Because of this I've often felt that perhaps God wanted to use me as a witness to the value of all life," Ramona says.

Sometimes the courage to act decisively springs from a deep well of personal conviction. To Ramona, for example, abortion was out of the question. To another person, even someone who has nurtured her beliefs over time, the courage to act on them may go missing at a critical moment, and can be re-won only with patience and struggle. This is true in the face of physical danger as much as it is in the face of a moral challenge.

No matter how it arises, every act of courage has the power to give birth to new ones, whether through the chain reaction of inspiration, or more directly. This was true in Ramona's case. Almost ten years earlier, in the same hospital, another mother had found out that she was carrying an anencephalic baby, and on hearing that this woman had decided to have her baby anyway, Ramona found extra confidence and a sense of peace. And the story isn't over yet: in the year since Isaiah's birth and death, Ramona's hospital has called on her to help counsel members of a support group for grieving women.

Anne, a cousin of mine, showed similar courage in following her heart, though the circumstances could not have been more different. Troubled by the endless conflict in the Middle East, she wished she could do more than read about it in the papers. So when an organization in the West Bank sent out a plea for help, she signed up and traveled to Bethlehem as a volunteer.

Anne knew she was heading into an extremely dangerous environment. Given the constant back-and-forth between the two opposing forces in the city — the Israeli Defense Force and the PLO — anyone or anything that moved was a potential target, especially at night. But what was the point of traveling to Bethlehem, if protecting oneself meant cowering indoors?

Once settled in her new quarters and working at her new job (she cares for blind and disabled women and children at a private group home) Anne began exploring the area around Bethlehem on foot, trying to get to know as many people as she could on both sides of the conflict, and listening to their perspectives.

Anne admits that life in a combat zone can be tense: she has witnessed gun battles and helicopter raids, and had to comfort traumatized survivors. She has met people who have resigned themselves to a war they believe will never end. But she also found pillars of resilience, strength, and hope — people who go on loving and giving, who offer coffee to a complete stranger, and beckon a foreigner in to share a meal.

At one point Anne weathered a 46-hour barrage of artillery fire between a nearby Jewish settlement and a Palestinian village. Another time, Israeli tanks moved into her neighborhood:

> Things are really getting out of hand here. It is absolutely crazy...Who knows who is shooting at whom? There have been countless shots right through our olive grove, twenty feet from my window. At one point last night something came whistling past, and right afterward there was a huge explosion on Hebron Road. My heart skipped a few beats. A little later there were more ear-piercing booms. As I watch, one red ball after another rises silently from the Israeli tanks in Beit Jala, each of them followed by a enormous cracking sound. One was fired from just three houses away...

I fell asleep while the battle continued, and slept all night, thanks to your prayers. One of the old ladies I care for is distressed that because of all this, she will not be able to get to the doctor any time soon. She had major surgery three weeks ago, and her antibiotics and pain medication ran out ten days ago.

Worried for her safety, I sent Anne an e-mail to ask how she was doing. Her reply surprised me, "I can't explain it, but I am happy and feel completely at peace. I truly believe that God hears our prayers, and that he will do as he wills. That gives me strength to go on living here. It might be that I will have to suffer, but I know I am in God's hands, and that means everything to me."

After several months in the West Bank, Anne returned home for a short breather. She was a changed person. Once timid and jittery, she was now relaxed; once taken with the little things of life – her houseplants, her cockatiels, and her classical music – she was now consumed by a much broader vision.

I never asked Anne about all this, or even commented on it, but she unwittingly explained it to me. During one particularly tense period, she said, she had sought refuge in Jerusalem, in the Garden of Gethsemane, and while there she had experienced something that altered her whole outlook on life:

I was lonely and exhausted, and I needed a quiet place to think. But once I got there, I forgot about myself — I was thinking of Jesus, and the agony he had suffered right where I was sitting. He felt forsaken, but he prayed, "Not my will, but Thy will." Somehow that gave me courage and strength, and I felt I would get through whatever might lie ahead.

Describing in his journal his own anxieties about death, Leo Tolstoy reveals a similar approach to overcoming them:

I like my garden, I like reading a book, I like caressing a child. By dying I lose all this, and therefore I do not wish to die, and I fear death. It may be that my whole life consists of such desires...and if that is so I cannot help being afraid of what will prevent their gratification. But if they have given way and been replaced in me by another desire the desire to do the will of God, to give myself to him in my present state and in any possible future state — then the more my desires have changed the less I fear death, and the less does death exist for me.

Anne is back in Israel as I write, working in a Bethlehem neighborhood patrolled by snipers and lit up at night by exploding shells. There are few foreigners left in the area. Yet she remains courageous. "I pray every day for protection," she said shortly before she returned. "And I know that many people are praying for me. Why should I worry? Won't all those prayers be heard?"

15

Healing

In 1933 my uncle Hardy, who was studying at Tübingen, met a fellow student, Edith, and fell in love with her. A year and a half later they married and settled at Silum, a tiny commune set high in the Alps. With matching poetic temperaments and a shared love of history and literature, the young couple could not have been better suited for each other, or happier, especially after Edith discovered that she was expecting a child. But their joy was not to last long.

Within days of the baby's birth, Edith developed childbed fever, then universally fatal. Soon the infection spread to her bloodstream. Her temperature rose, her pulse quickened, her veins became inflamed, and her body began to swell. She was dying, and there seemed to be no hope of recovery.

Hardy was not ready to let his young wife go, however, and nor was his father – my grandfather. As Edith's condition worsened, he gathered the members of Silum and led them in prayer on her behalf. He also laid his hands on her and asked God to heal her, if that was his will.

Edith slowly recovered, and at one point her doctor even pronounced her out of danger. Shortly after this, however, her fever returned and she lost ground again. One day she would feel better; the next, she would be critically ill.

It was around this time that my grandfather noticed something he hadn't before: that Edith's spirits seemed to fluctuate with her health, and that both went up or down according to the state of the close-knit group around her. When they were depressed or pessimistic or petty, she weakened tangibly; if they rallied around her with joy and resolve, she regained strength. It was as if her body had become a barometer for the atmosphere of the group.

Shaken by this mysterious phenomenon, the people at Silum prayed more persistently than ever. But their focus was not Edith's physical health. Rather, they sought to have their eyes opened in such a way that they could understand the spiritual nature of her struggle, and identify and remove every potential obstacle to victory, including their own personal agendas and opinions – and thus make way for God to heal them all, in body *and* soul. As my grandfather explained at the time, "There can be no victory of the Holy Spirit as long as people set themselves up as healers of sickness. The Spirit has nothing in common with magic. It *can* heal, but not until self-will and all other human claims to power disappear. Then and only then will the Spirit show itself as the spirit that heals sickness, drives out demons, and overcomes death." It was in this sense that Edith's illness was fought and, after a few weeks, finally overcome.

Remembering it all after many years, my parents, who had lived in Silum at the time, explained that Edith had seen her battle in terms of a larger, spiritual one – the battle between light and darkness, life and death. Because of this, she didn't fight just for her own sake, or for her family's sake. Obviously she wanted to live, but she also felt that if there was a victory to be won, it had to mean more than her own survival. It must be a living testimony to the power that is unleashed when people unite to pray for a common goal.

Six decades later, another relative of mine experienced the same healing power of prayer. It was a February day in 1996, and one of my nieces, who had married three years before, had just called my wife and me to announce the arrival of her first child. Simon was a beautiful, healthy, six-pound baby, perfect in every way – at least at first. But within hours, he developed difficulty breathing. Oxygen was brought, and an ambulance called (the birth had taken place at a rural clinic). On the way to the hospital, the baby turned blue.

Once there, X-rays soon confirmed what the doctors feared: both of Simon's lungs were badly infected. If he survived, they predicted, he would most likely sustain hearing loss and visual impairment, if not brain damage as well.

Struggling to shut out the doctors' words, and fearing that this was the beginning of the end, Simon's parents were numb with discouragement and grief. But not for long. Why not, they thought, turn to God and ask him to heal Simon? Why accept defeat? After all, God knew things Simon's doctors didn't. And Simon himself wasn't giving up. Beneath the maze of wires, needles, tubes, and lights, beneath the hum of the mechanical ventilator breathing for him, he was still kicking – fighting for life.

Simon's parents prayed, but his condition deteriorated. By evening he was bleeding from his lungs and needed a transfusion. Later the same night his blood pressure dropped. Dopamine, a powerful drug, was started, but still his life hung in the balance. Ten miles away, however, another force was being enlisted: the prayers of dozens of members of our church. It happened spontaneously, but quickly: as one person after another found out about

Simon, plans were made to gather and intercede on his behalf. Meanwhile, Simon's parents and a handful of friends continued to pray around the baby at the hospital.

At midnight, Simon suddenly turned a corner; by five A.M. the oxygen was turned down. His doctor, who had not left the baby all night, looked up, perplexed, and said, "My God, you people must know how to pray. I can't come up with any other explanation for why he's still here." Another doctor was more blunt. "Your child should have died," she said, shaking her head in disbelief.

Over the next days, despite a specialist's prediction of further obstacles, Simon improved so steadily that he was soon discharged. Today he is a healthy five-year-old, with no neurologic damage of any kind.

Simon's story, like Edith's, is a memorable testimony to the power of prayer. But despite their drama, neither story is unique. In fact, instances of recovery prompted by such intercession are so common today that healing and prayer are often spoken of in the same breath. They are also spoken of so casually, and so often sensationalized, that many people regard them with a justifiable mixture of skepticism and embarrassment.

Still, the biblical connection between prayer and healing, as spoken of in passages like the following one from the Gospel of Matthew, cannot be dismissed: "Ask, and it will be given to you; seek and you will find; knock, and the door will be opened to you. For everyone who asks receives; he who seeks finds; and to him who knocks, the door will be opened."

To someone who has experienced healing or witnessed it in another person, these words of Jesus are not a mere promise, but an undeniable reality. To someone who has not, on the other hand, they may arouse frustration. What about the spouse or parent or child who is prayed over day after day, but then dies anyway? What about the person who seems to have been healed, only to be snatched away later? (This happened to Edith, by the way: eight years after her brush with death, she died of a ruptured appendix.)

Reflecting on such questions, I have no answers. But I do have a few thoughts, the first being that to set one's hopes on miracles and wonders is to set oneself up for disappointment. Optimism is a powerful medicine, but it can't undo the laws of nature or the will of God. It is true that when we act in faith, miracles do occur. But as the Swedish thinker Dag Hammarskjöld once observed, the consequence is that in clinging to such happenings, we are "tempted to make miracles the ground for our hope...and thus lose the confidence of faith."

Further, no matter the apparent effectiveness (or ineffectiveness) of our prayers, I believe we should still turn to God and believe that he hears us. And in doing so we should not forget that though most of us habitually focus, in our prayers, on telling him our problems and desires, we might be more successful in discerning his will by becoming silent and letting *him* speak.

Finally, we should also realize that God may not respond to our prayers for healing in the way we expect him to, and that the questions we ask may not even be answerable in the way we want them to be. Writing in *A Grief Observed*, C. S. Lewis noted, "When I lay some questions before God I get no answer. But a rather special sort of 'No answer.' It is not the locked door. It is more like a silent, certainly not uncompassionate, gaze. As though He shook His head not in refusal but waiving the question. Like, 'Peace, child, you don't understand.'"

Lewis continues, "Can a mortal ask questions which God finds unanswerable? Quite easily, I should think… How many hours are there in a mile? Is yellow square or round? Probably half the questions we ask – half our great theological and metaphysical problems – are like that."

Given the modern tendency to believe that we can find a cure for every ailment, if we search hard enough, this is an important point to contemplate. In the realm of healing, for example, how can we be sure that the treatment is more important than the ailment? Where does one end and the other begin? Could it be that they are sometimes one and the same? When an arrogant, self-absorbed person has been brought low by misfortune or tragedy and turned into a humbler, more loving one, has he been harmed or healed? Perhaps we are too limited in our thinking, those of us who think of healing merely in physical terms.

That wholeness and healing can be found in death as well as in life is not hard to accept in the case of an elderly person who has lived life to the full and is ready to go. But the thought is valid, regardless of age. When Zach, a young man, was stricken with an aggressive cancer, his congregation prayed that God might heal him and bring him back to health. Zach received top-notch medical care at a local university hospital, and for several months he defied the odds and bolstered his supporters' confidence. At one point he was even pronounced in remission. Then, about a month later, he suddenly took a downturn. In a matter of weeks he was gone.

Speaking with Zach and his family shortly before he died, I sensed that their church's continuous prayers for healing, while sincere, had not necessarily lessened their ordeal – and had made it even harder at times. How should they react, for instance, when well-meaning friends insisted that Zach would pull through, when their gut feelings told them that the opposite was true? Should they just play along – "trust in God" and pretend to believe what they couldn't? Not knowing what to think, I blurted out something like, "Well, Zach, are you ready for *whatever* happens – not just ready to be physically healed, but also ready to die?" My point was that the whole question of recovering or being cured wasn't getting him anywhere. His cancer was now so advanced that he surely didn't have more than a week or two left. There was no time for distractions...

After an intense struggle, Zach decided that what he really needed to do was face the fact that he was dying, and honestly and unconditionally accept God's will for him, whatever it might be. In the days that followed, he continued to slide downhill, but it no longer mattered to him. He was dying: there was no denying that. But he was also – paradoxical as it sounds – experiencing the healing that had evaded him for so long.

Inwardly, Zach was undergoing an unmistakable change. He became less self-conscious, he reached out more to other people; he mellowed and deepened. Most remarkable for this once confident, argumentative twenty-something, he began to reflect the childlike spirit Jesus says each of us must find if we are to enter the kingdom of God.

Zach's transformation did not come easily, or without a price. Nor did the healing he found make saying goodbye any easier. For his mother in particular, it was still unspeakably hard: "When you lose someone you're close to, especially if you're right there with him when he goes, the hurt and the shock are indescribably deep. I just don't know how we got through it." Even so, she agreed with her husband, who said, "There is no way Zach's death was a defeat. It's true his cancer wasn't successfully treated. But he found peace of heart, and in that sense he *was* healed."

Despite their grief, there was a healing of sorts for Zach's parents too. As his father said afterward, "Life still has its ups and downs. Some days we fall apart; other days we do okay. But being with our son on the final night of his life changed us. We finally saw that death need not be a frightening thing. It may be the last enemy, but it's not the end of the story."

16

Caring

Karl, eighty-nine, was a rebel against old age, and it didn't make caring for him easy. He could get upset with you when you didn't let him walk alone (it wasn't safe), or when he couldn't hear what you were saying (he was nearly deaf). Still, everyone loved him dearly. When his nurse pushed him through the neighborhood in his wheelchair, people stopped what they were doing to come over and say hello. Children left their play and ran over, showing him dandelions, shaking his hand, telling him their secrets. *"Ja, Ja,"* he would say happily, in his thick German accent, though he didn't understand a word. Teenagers loved him too, because despite his age, he was "with it." He read the papers and knew what was going on, and he was keenly interested in what they were reading and what they thought about current events.

Karl never took the love that he received for granted. Given his rocky childhood, which opened with the death of his mother and ended when he ran away from his violently abusive father, that wasn't surprising. What *was* remarkable was the way his own gruff exterior fell away as he approached the final days of his life. Sometimes, on being tucked into bed, he would even apologize to his caregivers (who included children and grandchildren) for having been abrupt earlier in the day. "I am sorry I was angry. Please forgive me." He died peacefully at ninety, surrounded by his family and by Irma, his wife of almost seventy years.

At first glance Karl's old age seems ordinary enough – a picture-perfect example of how life ought to be in the so-called golden years. But while every elderly person deserves the care that he was fortunate to enjoy, most do not in fact receive it. Sadly, the most common scenario involves confinement and fear, an eternally flickering television set to ward off loneliness and silence, and – despite Social Security – more poverty than any other age group in the population.

Only two or three generations ago, many people lived out their lives in one place. They raised their children, grew old, and died in their homes, surrounded by family and friends and church. In most sectors of society today – marked as it is by mobility and rootlessness – the sense of belonging to a particular community has been lost. Nowadays, for whatever reason, aging parents often lose what few close connections they have with their children by mid-life and enter old age in loneliness.

A young woman I know says that in the nursing home where she used to work, it was not unusual for a dying client's family to instruct the staff not to call during the night. "Don't call me while I'm sleeping," one man told her when she called to say that his father might die during the night. "Give me a ring in the morning, if you have to."

Such callousness may be extreme, but its causes are pervasive: estrangement, isolation, and long periods of physical separation. After visiting the United States in the mid-1990s, Mother Teresa spoke of her shock at seeing how our country tends to warehouse its elderly. While noting that in one place she visited, they seemed to have no material lack – food, medicine, nurses, comfortable furniture, entertainment, and the like – she also described their bored, blank stares and their gaping mouths, their resignation, and the way some kept glancing toward the door. "Sister told me," she said, "that this is the way it is nearly every day. They are waiting, hoping that a son or daughter will come to visit them. They are hurt because they have been forgotten."

The plight of the institutionalized elderly seems simple enough to pinpoint, but it has many deep-going roots and defies a simple solution. Talk to anyone with an aging parent, especially one who is no longer capable of living independently, and the complexity of the issue will quickly become clear. No one wants their mother or father to die unloved, in an unkempt, impersonal environment, but when you add up the commitments that keep a working adult tied down from dawn to dusk, it's perfectly understandable why so few find it possible to provide long-term home care for their parents. Most lack money, time, space, or energy – if not all four.

Aging at home isn't all roses either, especially for people who live alone. And even when circumstances allow a family to care for a loved one in their own house, there are numerous challenges, as Joan – an acquaintance with a bedridden father – confesses:

> For someone who's never experienced it firsthand, it's hard to imagine what actually transpires in a household when a member becomes terminally ill. I don't live at home – I have my own house and family – but I spend time with my father whenever I can, and it has given me some idea of just what caring means.

There was no exact moment when Dad crossed from being merely old and sick with pneumonia to being "terminal" – it happened only gradually. Days of illness stretched into weeks, and then months, and though we were always wondering when he'd turn a corner, he didn't. He'd start to pick up, but then his fever would recur and send him on the next round of antibiotics.

Finally we realized that things had gone on far too long, and arranged for home nursing care twenty-four hours a day. He declined rapidly, weakening to the point where his doctor told him it might be the end. Our minds struggled to grasp what was happening. Where were the intimate moments of farewell I'd imagined to be part of a death? Privacy seemed a thing of the past, and I chafed under the need to relate to an ever-present nurse. How could I tell Dad in words how much he'd meant to me? And wouldn't that be admitting the truth of what his doctor had said? I shed my tears in private.

We groped to adjust, as relationships in our family kaleidoscoped dizzily. There was Mom's role reversal: before, Dad had always looked out for her; now he depended on her to look after him. A hospital bed in a separate room replaced the bed they'd shared for fifty-odd years, and everywhere you turned were spittoons, oxygen wires, glasses of water sporting straws, and dishes of barely-touched food.

With doctor's appointments, blood tests, bed changes, and baths, there seemed few hours of the day where Dad could be truly peaceful. And besides these outer distractions, he was constantly short of breath. Comfort eluded him, and he was always fussing with sheets, pillows, and leg positions. Nothing I could do seemed to relieve him, and it was a rare respite when Dad could slip into anything deeper than a restless doze.

Dad did not die. He hung on, but recovery has not been quick to follow. Though physically somewhat stronger now, he still requires 24-hour care, and his once keen interest in life has been hard to rekindle. His doctor's repeated assurances that recovery will come with time have begun to sound empty.

Before his illness, Dad was always used to being in control of his life. Now it's just a small world, but he's still very much in charge: if you want to take him for a ride, it's too cold; if his nurse disappears for a few moments, he watches the clock for his return; if it's three in the morning and he thinks it's time for his morning shower, it's impossible to get him back to sleep. One day I tried to put lotion on his dry, scaly skin. "Too greasy," he said, so I put the bottle away. As time goes on, I've had to come to terms with being unable to undo his pain, and to trust that my presence will somehow convey what I cannot accomplish through actions...

Joan feels privileged to help care for her father. But she admits that she does feel hopelessly inadequate at times, and she is certain that without the bonds of love that keep a family together, the unavoidable tensions would soon create cracks, if not deep fissures.

Given the challenges that arise in such situations, it is easy to see why families who start out caring for someone at home often end up turning to a nursing home or hospice. That is nothing to be ashamed of: anyone who has cared for someone with a chronic condition knows that eventually it takes a toll. Yet just as the most menial chore can become a privilege, if performed with love, so too, a difficult decision can be made bearable if it is made with compassion and sensitivity.

Tragically, both are often lacking, or present only in words, and the result is that many elderly people feel unwanted and abandoned. Is it any wonder that large numbers feel they are a burden on their families; that many who retire soon tire of living, and that it is no longer taboo, but commonplace, to speak of a terminally ill person's "right" to die? How many people would fight for such a thing, if they were guaranteed a right to decent end-of-life care — a right to be loved?

An article recently sent to me from England quotes a doctor who excused himself from charges of physician-assisted suicide by claiming, "It could have taken another week before she died, and I needed the bed." In this country, too, such incidents are no longer unheard of. This is especially tragic when one considers how much every elderly person has to give, no matter how frail, incapacitated, or disoriented he is. Even a senile person can

contribute something by his presence, if those around him
have the patience and humility to receive it.

As a schoolboy in the Paraguayan village where I grew
up, I used to help Bernard in the stables where he
worked. Bernard had a way with horses and seemed
strong as an ox — reason enough to make him one of my
boyhood heroes. Decades later, as a seventy-five-year
old, I got to know him again in a very different way.
Once a gifted man with a wide variety of interests (aside
from his affinity with animals, he was an avid gardener
with an impressive knowledge of chemistry and biol-
ogy), he was now suffering the first ravages of
Alzheimer's disease and slowly, irreversibly losing all his
skills and faculties.

As Bernard's illness progressed, his frustration grew:
he lost his ability to do simple things like make tea; his
sense of direction failed him; he had no idea what day it
was, or what time. Soon he could not even communicate
his most basic needs — though one only had to read his
eyes to feel his pain. Toward the end he could no longer
recognize his own family — not even Eileen, his wife of
fifty years. But Bernard never lost his smile — a broad,
slow grin that lit up his face as if something happy had
just dawned on him. And he never lost his love for

children. In fact, he saved his last smile for a baby a neighbor brought by.

Like Bernard, my mother-in-law, Margrit, was completely incapacitated by the time she died: she suffered from Lou Gehrig's disease for the last thirteen years of her life; for eight of those she was basically bedridden.

Blessed with eleven children, and more than sixty grandchildren, Margrit was a tireless worker who had a knack for getting things done. She was a talented woman too, as was obvious to anyone who heard her direct a choir or lead an orchestra (she had studied the violin at a prestigious European conservatory). Still, when I think of her, I think of the German saying, "quiet waters run deep." In contrast to her husband, an animated talker, she was so unassuming that when asked for her opinion on something, she was known to smile and say only, "I'm listening." But it was not because she was timid. In fact, there was a confidence and sureness about her that spoke louder than words.

To me, Margrit's last years highlight the significance of caring for the elderly, and not just in the sense of helping or nursing them, but in learning to be attentive to the gifts they give back. While another musician might have lamented the erosion of her skills, she did not; on the contrary, she meekly accepted her limits. Eventually she became so frail that she could speak only with great effort.

She could no longer do anything for herself. But she still took visitors' hands in her own faltering clasp; and she still spoke to them, even if silently, with her loving gaze. And, as she whispered to a nurse one day, "I can still pray." Through all this, she reminded us that in contrast to the proud achievements of youth, there is something about the simplicity of love that time can never destroy.

No matter the age or condition of a dying person, I believe that every one possesses a spark of such love. It may be hidden, or hard to find. But if we truly care, we will not give up looking for it. And once we have uncovered it, we will fan it into flame and nurture it until the end.

17

Dying

Even in his late eighties, my wife's father, Hans, made trips from Connecticut to Europe. A self-taught scholar with a passion for history and religion, he wasn't going to let age get in the way of conferences and tours. If meeting interesting people required flying long distances, so be it. After all, traveling didn't wear him out. It rejuvenated him. A family member predicted, "When he dies, he'll die in harness."

On Christmas Eve, 1992, at the age of ninety, Hans was sitting on a hay bale, a shepherd's cloak over his shoulders and a wooden staff in his hand, having volunteered to join in an outdoor nativity pageant. Feeling cold, he asked to be taken indoors, and soon someone was driving him home, just a stone's throw away. But

Hans never made it. Opening the car door for him after the ride, his driver found that he was no longer alive.

To lose a friend or family member unexpectedly is always a shock. Yet if he or she is elderly, and has lived a fulfilled life, it can also be a blessing. Surely most people, if they were allowed to choose, would elect to die as Hans did – happily and quickly. But few go that way. For most, the end comes gradually.

Dying almost always involves a hard struggle. Part of it is fear, which is often rooted in uncertainty of the unknown and unknowable future. Part of it may be the urge to fulfill unmet obligations or to be relieved of past regrets or guilt. But part of it is also our natural resistance to the thought that everything we know is coming to an end. Call it survival instinct, the will to live, or whatever – it is a powerful primal force. And except in rare cases (those who die in a heavily medicated state, for instance) it can give a person amazing resilience.

Maureen, an old friend in her mid-nineties, fell and broke her hip two years ago; since then her younger sister has died, and so has one of her sons. She herself is bedridden much of the day, and confined to a wheelchair the rest of the time. Still, this "tough old bird" (as she calls herself) who likes to shock visitors by sneaking a rubber mouse into their coffee, has more sparkle than many people half her age. Having met her previous goal of reaching the year 2000, she now jokes that she's planning to stick around until she's 100. And in resisting old age with every fiber of her being, she has literally kept herself alive.

Then there is Esther, the stepdaughter of one of my sisters, who was diagnosed with an aggressive cancer when she was ten. Within days this lively girl who loved to skip rope, play tag, and go horse riding with her father found herself confined to a bed. Soon afterward one of her legs had to be amputated. Esther wept, then pulled herself together and asked for a prosthesis. "I'll be walking by Christmas – just wait and see," she promised. Later she went blind. Again she refused to be cowed, and spoke of continuing to take piano lessons anyway. Cheerful and plucky, she didn't die of cancer so much as fight it until the end.

With the will to live, a person can overcome unbelievable odds. But death cannot be forestalled forever, and eventually physical life must draw to a close. Strangely, our culture resists this truth. In Florida, thousands of the elderly congregate in retirement communities where they dance, date, exercise, and sunbathe – and pay exorbitant amounts for facelifts to keep up the appearance of perpetual youth. No one would begrudge the aged a chance to have fun or "live life to the full." But at the same time there is something disturbing about acting like you're twenty when you're really seventy – as if such a pretense could stave off wrinkles and heart disease, incontinence and memory loss.

In past centuries plague and famine decimated whole towns and cities, and sooner or later every family was touched by a woman's death in childbirth, or the loss of a baby. As writer Philip Yancey points out, "No one could live as if death did not exist." Nowadays, thanks to modern medicine, improved nutrition, public sanitation, and greater life expectancy, death no longer seems such an unavoidable reality. And when we can't avoid it, we try to hide it. To quote Yancey again, "Health clubs are a booming industry, as are nutrition and health food stores. We treat physical health like a religion. Meanwhile we wall off death's blunt reminders – mortuaries, intensive care units, cemeteries."

In maintaining such taboos, we have largely removed death from our day-to-day experience. But there is a flip side: we have also lost the ability to accept the end of life when it does finally come. I do not mean that we should belittle a dying person's fears by coaxing him to accept death as a friend, as some experts do. There is good reason to view death as an enemy, which is the way the Bible describes it. Like the writer of the Psalms, who begs for God's hand to steady him as he goes through the "valley of the shadow of death," most people do not look forward to dying, but are apprehensive about it. Even my uncle Herman, though he died confidently, struggled to get to that point and admitted his fear that it would be like entering a long, dark tunnel.

Much has been written on how to comfort the terminally ill, but it should be remembered that each individual has unique needs and desires. One person will be talkative and nervous, the next quiet and sullen, the next completely distraught. One will be depressed, another will try to bargain with God, still another will be calm. These are all normal responses, and none of them is right or wrong. After all, dying is a complex process and involves the entire tangled spectrum of human emotions – dread, anxiety and exhaustion; hope and relief. And these feelings affect not only the dying, but those around him too.

It is important to consider a dying person's surroundings. A hospital may be best for recovering from surgery, but it is hardly the ideal place to die. For one thing, it cannot possibly match the familiarity and comfort of a home; for another, visiting hours do not allow for the spontaneous coming and going of close friends and family members.

Sometimes the choice between home and hospital is excruciatingly difficult. One person will find the environment of a hi-tech intensive care unit reassuring; for another, the maze of wires and IV lines and the constant bleeping of electronic monitors is so disruptive that it prevents sleep. Either way, it is vital to try to discern a dying person's wishes and to communicate them to the attending physician, even if they go against our own gut feelings, and even at the risk of being misunderstood. Medical technology has made great advances in recent years, but beyond a certain point it may prolong dying, instead of extending life. The line between the two is often very fine.

Naturally, a private setting is no guarantee of a peaceful death. When adult children who have not lived together for years gather at the home of a dying parent, they just as often clash as harmonize. And when wills and inheritances are involved, even carefully hidden tensions may explode into the open. All the more it is important that when we enter the room of someone who is near death, we are aware of his need for peace, and respect it. It cannot be said strongly enough: a deathbed is no place to bring up old grievances. Nor is it the place to belatedly press for reconciliation.

It is different if the dying person feels the need to re-solve something, or if we can set something right by of-fering a simple apology. According to hospice nurse Maggie Callanan, co-author of the book *Final Gifts,* the emotional needs of the dying are often more painful than their physical ailments, and the failure to address them can leave them so unsettled that they feel unable to die. Remembering a dying Vietnam vet she once helped, she writes:

> One day I received an urgent call from the nurse on duty.
> "Please get here fast," she said. "Everything seemed to be going okay, but now Gus is very confused and anxious, and we're losing it."
> "No, I bet we're finally getting it," I thought to myself. I had wondered how long Gus would be able to keep up the tough-guy façade. I felt there must be times he felt frightened – even if he wouldn't talk about it, or allow his fear to show.
> The scene was chaotic. Gus was crying out in anguish; his speech was so disjointed it was hard to make any sense of it. But in his confused language were the words "vil-lages," "babies," "napalm," "burning" – and the tragic words "I did it, I did it!"

Eventually, Gus's caregivers figured out that he wanted to see a chaplain – a request they were happy to meet. Shortly afterward, Gus died, relieved at having been able to unburden himself to a local priest.

Sometimes the distress of the dying is rooted in the worry that no one knows what they are going through — or that they are about to go. This fear may be present even in people who are surrounded by a large circle of friends or family members. To quote *Final Gifts* once more:

> Many dying people are lonely, not only because people don't visit, but also because of what happens when people *do* visit. Visitors may spend their time with the person wrapped up in idle talk about the weather, sports, or politics. Perhaps because, consciously or unconsciously, it's intended to do so, their chatter keeps the dying person from being able to speak intimately. A dying person's world shrinks, narrowing to a few important relationships and the progress of his illness. When dying people aren't allowed to talk about what's happening to them, they become lonely, even amid loving, concerned people. They may feel isolated and abandoned, and in turn become resentful and angry.

Small talk and humor have a place alongside prayers, of course; there is nothing more oppressive than unnatural holiness. But far more significant than words are simple deeds of love: a cloth offered to cool a burning forehead, a hand reached out to steady a shaking shoulder, ointment to moisten dry lips. Though modest, such acts of kindness are all most people want or need at the end. Helen Prejean, a nun who has accompanied prison inmates to their deaths, notes that even when there is nothing else you can do for a dying person, you can make sure that the last face he sees comforts him with eyes of love.

Unfortunately, the dying often take their last breaths alone. Sometimes a person appears to be slipping away, but hangs on for weeks or months. In other cases, a person may seem to be on the mend, only to surprise everyone by dying suddenly. Interestingly, hospice workers have found that when a person is worried that his death might distress loved ones, he may try to spare them by waiting until he is alone, and only then breathing his last.

On the day that Rob, an old friend, died a few years ago, he called his wife and children to his room, told them each how much he loved them, and wished them well for the future. Hours later he was gone. Brad, another friend, was unable to say goodbye. When he fell ill, his children (all adults) traveled long distances to see him one more time. One of them always remained at his bedside, ready to call the others at a moment's notice. When the end came, however, it came so quickly that most of his children were not in the house. All were deeply disappointed, and some even felt guilty.

In trying to help this family through their grief, I reassured them that whether or not we are there, no one is truly alone at the hour of death. On the contrary, I believe that the dying are always in God's hands.

Dying

Recalling the last night he spent with a patient who died of cancer, a doctor I know wrote in his journal:

Although intermittently confused, Mark made several lucid comments between labored breaths. At one point he said something about "going" somewhere, and I replied, "Yes, you can go, Jesus will take you!"

"But it's so hard!" he responded.

I said, "Don't cling to us. Cling to God!"

"I'm trying," he said, "but I don't know what to do next. It's so unfamiliar!"

"Yes, but you are going before us," his mother said. "And then you can tell us how to get there."

Later Mark asked his father to read something from the Bible, which he did. Just as he was finishing Romans 8, Mark said, "Maybe Jesus will come!" Several of us responded, "He *will* come!"

Later he said quite loudly, "Can't wait much longer!"

Over the next half hour, Mark's breathing became more labored, though every few minutes he would say something. Sometimes it was just one word; sometimes a whole sentence, but hurriedly spoken between gasps, and hard to understand. His eyes were open, but he didn't seem to see us any more: "This is a great struggle...You don't know how tired I am! Pathetic...Don't focus on...but on the spiritual." And later: "Gotta go...Jesus...Amazing! Very real..."

After a pause, he added "I feel real bad, but I can't do anything about it now." We assured him that whatever he regretted, he was forgiven; that God would take him; and that it would be very soon. Mark then asked for water, and said, "Gonna go very shortly...One of my best days..."

About an hour and a half later, he took his last breath.

As Mark's story shows, dying is a mystery before which we can do little but stand in awe. If someone is fighting for life, we can uphold him and fight with him; if he seems ready to die, we can assure him that we understand, and release him. Beyond that, however, we must get out of the way. I say this because ultimately, nothing is more crucial at the bed of a dying person than an atmosphere of peace. And as long as we focus on ourselves and our attempts to ease his pain, we risk disrupting and distracting him, and preventing him from finding this peace.

When life draws to a close, *everything* — no matter how important it once seemed to be — falls away. And when it is gone, nothing matters but the state of the soul. We cannot look into a person's heart; nor is it our place to worry about how he stands before God. But in opening our eyes and ears to what he is going through, we can share his suffering by letting it become ours, and we can pray that he finds mercy and grace. Finally, we must let the dying go, trusting, as Henri Nouwen puts it, "that death does not have the last word. We can look at them...and give them hope; we can hold their bodies in our arms. And we can trust that mightier arms than ours will receive them and give them the peace and joy they desire."

18

Grief

No matter the circumstances when someone dies, we tend to haul out the same old clichés. Part of it is probably our fear of hurting someone by saying "the wrong thing." Part of it is that we are so overwhelmed by emotions that we don't know what we really think. But a good part of it is also our general discomfort with grief.

For most of us, the raw reality of losing someone (or seeing someone else suffer such a loss) is too much for us to address honestly and fully. It demands vulnerability – the admission of weakness, dependence, and the fear that we've come to the end of our rope – and because of this we try to brush it off, or skirt it by means of pat phrases. And when that doesn't work we treat it like a speed bump: slowing down because we have to, but then hurrying on as quickly as possible.

Sometimes we do this for ourselves, in the hope that if we can pick ourselves up again and "move on," we can limit our pain. Sometimes, worried what others will think about us if we don't pull ourselves together soon, we mask our pain by bottling it up silently.

Common as it is to try to deal with grief in this way, it does not work. Hide it, talk around it, postpone it, pretend it isn't there – in the long run, grief will never go away until it is met head on and allowed to run its course. Given the unique circumstances that shape every loss, the time this takes will vary with every person. Tragically, time isn't always granted, as Gina, a young woman I know, found out.

When Tom, Gina's sixteen-year-old brother, died of an overdose several years ago, she was devastated. "In a way, I'm still not through dealing with it," she says. Friends and acquaintances were sympathetic at first, but after a while they grew tired of her inability to "move on" and made her feel guilty that she was still struggling:

> I tried to explain, but they never really understood me. It seemed like they expected my life to be "normal" again. I often went through times of sadness, bitterness, and other painful emotions, but people were uncomfortable with this. I was so alone.

Grief

Six months after Tom's death, a good friend of his died. I felt so much pain. But when I told one of my friends how I was feeling, he said he was worried for me. He thought I should have been over "all of that" by now — which pressured me to feel the same.

I feel like I mourned my brother and his friend in isolation and confusion. I tried to gain meaning from their deaths, but it was very hard. Everyone just kept talking about how they shouldn't have died.

In a recent book of interviews on death and dying, author Studs Terkel recounts a conversation he had with Myra, a woman who experienced the same lack of empathy after her mother's death. She felt she had a right to grieve, but that other people's expectations kept taking it away from her. Saying she felt "disenfranchised," Myra explained:

> It means you're not supposed to feel grief, and not supposed to show it. I was in my late fifties when my mother died. She was eighty-one. People came up with the usual platitudes. "After all, she lived a good life." "You shouldn't feel so full of grief." But that's bullshit. That's why we can't handle death very well. We want a sort of drive-by grieving. Nobody wants you to carry on about it. They want you to deposit it like you do in a bank.

No wonder so many people feel they need to get over their grief quickly — and nobly to boot. Most will find this impossible to do; and in my experience, even those who succeed in hardening themselves so as to emerge intact will find out sooner or later that they cannot truly heal without allowing themselves time to grieve. After all, grief is the innate urge to go on loving someone who is no longer there, and to be loved back. And insofar as we hold ourselves back (or allow someone else to hold us back) from bringing this urge to expression, we will remain frustrated, and we will never heal. In other words, grief is the soul's natural response to loss, and should not be repressed. Writer Anne Morrow Lindbergh, whose son was kidnapped and killed when he was a baby, advises:

> One must grieve, and one must go through periods of numbness that are harder to bear than grief. One must refuse the easy escapes offered by habit and human tradition. The first and most common offerings of family and friends are always distractions ("Take her out" – "Get her away" – "Change the scene" – "Bring in people to cheer her up" – "Don't let her sit and mourn") when it is mourning one needs.
>
> Courage is a first step, but simply to bear the blow bravely is not enough. Stoicism is courageous, but it is only a halfway house on the long road. It is a shield, permissible for a short time only. In the end one has to discard shields and remain open and vulnerable. Otherwise, scar tissue will seal off the wound and no growth will follow.

It may sound cruel to advise a grieving person, as Lindbergh does, to remain open to further pain. After all, most of us instinctively protect ourselves, once wounded, by retreating from the fray. And it isn't easy to resist that temptation. Yet I have seen that when a person willingly submits to grief, it may act as a crucible that transforms. There is a catch, of course: the need for humility. Accepted only grudgingly, grief ends in resentment, bitterness, loneliness, and rebellion. Borne with humility, however, it empties the soul of its own agendas for healing, cleanses it of self-sufficiency, and allows room for something new.

For the parents of Matt, the young man whose story I told at the beginning of this book, grief became an occasion for self-examination and prayer and brought them close to each other and to God. As Matt's father, Randy, said shortly after his son's death, "It's a great temptation to throw myself back into my work, my daily rhythm, or whatever. But I can't do that if I'm going to gain anything from going through all this. God spoke through Matt's illness and death, and I don't want to 'get over it.' I want to be challenged and changed for the rest of my life."

Traditionally, the first step of grieving is preparing the body for viewing, and then for burial or cremation, and for Matt's brother, Nick, this was an important step in coming to terms with his loss:

> Grieving is hard, but it can bring you together with other people. My dad and I helped dress Matt after he died, and Matt's doctor made us feel that we could help, although he said we didn't have to if we'd rather not. It was good to be incorporated into things instead of stepping back and watching everything happen. I think you end up feeling numb when you're just an observer.
>
> It was scary to put on Matt's clothes and to feel his limp body, but at the same time I wouldn't have missed it. It was the last service – the last act of love – I could do for him.
>
> If you just walk away from a death, there's not much more you can say than, "Wow, what just happened?" But if you can say, "I did something, and I *know* what I just did," it has meaning.

Nick notes that grief can be a source of community, and I can attest that this is true. Take memorial services and funerals, for instance – they are not only painful, but healing, for the bereaved. There is a simple reason for this: by inviting friends and relatives to participate in viewing the body of someone we love and then laying it to rest in a cemetery or other place of burial, we are allowing them to share our pain.

Unfortunately, such age-old customs are disappearing, and not only because of pragmatic considerations, but because there is a dwindling appreciation for their symbolic power. Speaking of changing practices in his rural Midwestern hometown, author W. Paul Jones writes:

> More and more obituary notices indicate cremation, *without any service*. Even here in the Ozark Hills, many of the dead no longer have a special place...The mortician told me that the disposal of the ashes is usually left to him, to be scattered whenever and wherever he finds convenient. He uses them to fertilize his roses.

I have read of similar trends elsewhere, too: in several European cities, growing numbers are choosing to be buried (or otherwise disposed of) anonymously – and without any ceremonial farewell whatsoever.

Admittedly, funerals can place a great strain on families whose finances are already stretched. But one wonders how often money is really the limiting factor. What about those who leave plenty, but request no service and no marked grave? Do they regard themselves as burdens, or feel that they were only tolerated and not truly loved? What is it that they lack the natural desire to be remembered at least somehow, by somebody, after they are gone – or that they even wish to be forgotten?

Every family must find its own way to take leave of the dead, and I am not suggesting that one way is better than the other. How could it be, when cultural and religious backgrounds vary so widely that what one person finds deeply meaningful, another finds irreverent or distasteful? All the same, I believe that every human being has an innate need to know that he belongs to someone, and that he is cherished, and because of this I feel certain that no matter the circumstances of death, each one deserves the dignity of a loving farewell.

When New York's Twin Towers collapsed on September 11, 2001, thousands of grieving families were left with nothing but the knowledge that their loved ones were surely dead – for most there was no body to grieve over, nor even any concrete evidence of death. There were only holes: unopened mail, a vacant place at the table, an empty bed. It was all the more touching, then, that during a memorial service held in Lower Manhattan several weeks later, each family who attended was given a vial of earth from the site. More than a symbolic gesture, this gave the bereaved something to hold in their hands, and to bury or save.

Everyone responds differently to the challenges of loss. Sometimes expectations clash even in the same family. Not long after my mother died, for instance, my sisters and I were sitting at home with my father, having coffee. We were talking about our families, and having a good time. Papa, however, was hurt by our laughter and wanted to know how we could let life return to normal so quickly. Couldn't we see that he was still grieving for Mama? And why weren't we taking her death just as seriously?

Surely the return to "normalcy" is a vital step toward healing. But what I learned that day was the importance of respecting the pain of those who heal more slowly than those around them. Randy, above, spoke of the temptation to get back to work as soon as possible, an urge that seems understandable enough. Many people say their grief would drive them insane, if they didn't have a job. They need something, anything, to force them out of the house each day and keep them going.

But there are just as many who do not share this point of view at all. Unable to cope with the obligations of previous schedules and commitments, they cannot conceive of returning to "business as usual" while still deep in grief: to do that would be to admit that their mourning is over, when in fact it has just begun. And when they do finally pick up the pieces and look for a new focus in their lives, they may find that emerging from grief is no easier than grieving itself. In her memoir *Go Toward the Light*, Chris Oyler, whose eleven-year-old died after contracting AIDS through a blood transfusion, writes:

I'd like to say that I found solace enough in my husband and other boys. But that wasn't really true...What I realized soon after Ben's death was that I had to get to know my own children and my husband all over again. We had learned to function in crisis, learned to love each other through tears. But now we had to learn how to function all over again in normal times, when alarm clocks went off in the morning and there was homework to do at night.

Grieving families often find comfort in making connections with other bereaved people. Part of it may be the knowledge that those they are reaching out to know what they are going through, and will be sensitive to it; but part of it is also the satisfaction that comes from giving back after one has been on the receiving end of condolences and other forms of sympathy.

Several months after the death of Merrill, whose story I told in an earlier chapter, his wife, Kathy, traveled to another state to support a woman who had just lost her husband. Kathy told me later that instead of reviving her pain, this experience helped her to put it in perspective.

Sidney and Marjorie, another couple, lost their first son when he was only five weeks old; the day after he was buried, they took a severely abused foster child into their home. Others wondered how they would cope, but Marjorie says the boy gave them an outlet for the love they would have gone on lavishing on their baby, had he lived.

After Delf, a former teacher of mine, accidentally ran over his two-year-old son, killing him, he and his wife went through their neighborhood from house to house, sharing their pain and grief. Some time later they brought their child's clothes and toys to a poor couple in their neighborhood who had a child the same age.

Not everyone is able to turn grief into an occasion for healing. After losing their son, a couple I know drove several hours to meet another couple (I'll call them the Smiths) who had just lost a daughter in similar circumstances, and took them out for lunch. Sadly, the Smiths were so paralyzed by their pain that they were unable – unwilling, even – to see beyond it. Afraid that the other couple's loss would be too much to carry on top of their own, they did not even acknowledge their hosts' kindness, but gave them a cold shoulder.

Someone who has not suffered the death of a loved one might be tempted to write off a couple like the Smiths as self-centered. But that would be heartless. Deeply wounded people often spurn expressions of sympathy that they would otherwise accept, and sometimes they may even take themselves by surprise. It is not our place to judge.

In the same vein, it is presumptuous to offer quick explanations. Writing of September 11, 2001, Ellyn Spragins notes that because of the public nature of the catastrophes in New York and Washington, millions across the country, including people who live far away, grieved for the dead in the following weeks. "We've all prayed," she writes in the *New York Times*; "we've wept, learned the names of some of those who died, given blood, and sent money to charities…The suffering of strangers has become a part of our own lives." And yet, she notes, we're still at a loss: "How does pain depart? How do people heal? It feels disrespectful, insulting even, to frame an answer."

It is also risky. For one thing, the most compassionate advice may be misinterpreted as belittling; for another, it may cramp the person it was intended to console. How is a mother supposed to respond when, after having lost a baby, someone helpfully assures her that God "must have needed another angel"? The first thing most grieving people need is an arm around their shoulders, and permission to cry.

An acquaintance recently told me that after her mother died, she went to my parents, sobbing, and poured out her need. They listened, and listened more. Finally my father said quietly, "I understand." That was all. But it meant more to her than all the words of wisdom other people had given her.

When Linda's son, Matt, lay dying of cancer, she came across a book in which Henri Nouwen writes that "a caring silence can enter deeper into our memory than many caring words" – and found that it struck a chord. Just the previous summer, she and her husband had spent several days with Brad and Misty Bernall, whose daughter Cassie was killed in the infamous Columbine High School massacre of April 1999.

Speaking of the time she spent visiting Misty, Linda remembers the frustration of trying to comfort her while wondering what she was going through. "There was a lot of silence between us," she recalls. "At times I could see the need for it; at other times I worried that she was upset with me." Now Linda understands Misty's inability to chatter: "Because there just aren't any words that will make you feel better, silence is often what you want and need most. It heals." She goes on:

A year later, during Matt's last months, I knew Misty was thinking of me, and I knew she was hurting – for herself again, and for me. There were no words between us, but I felt close to her in our silence. A few times I picked up the phone to call her, but then couldn't. There wasn't anything to say. If I could have seen her, there would have been tears, but I don't think there would have been any words.

Three weeks after Matt died, Brad and Misty sent us a beautiful flower arrangement, with a card saying "We're praying for you." I thought of how hard it must have been for her to call the florist, and on the spur of the moment, I decided to call and thank her. I thought I'd be okay on the phone this time.

I called and got her voice mail, so I said, "Hi, Misty, this is Linda. Thanks for the flowers. I love you." Then I broke down. Her pain – my pain – what was there to say? I choked and quickly hung up.

The day before Matt died, Linda spent a long time in her living room, sitting quietly on the couch with a friend. A few days later, the same friend came back with another woman, and the three of them held hands as the tears trickled down their cheeks. "There is nothing more special than being with someone in total silence and knowing that you feel each other's hurt," says Linda. "It is an expression of deep love."

Generalizations are rarely helpful, but there is one thing about grief that can be safely said for everyone: it can never be passed over quickly. Grieving takes time and space – time to grasp the irreversible change of losing someone you love, and space to sort out your conflicting emotions.

Some people experience a surprising strength in the first days after a death; but even these soon feel the full impact of their loss. How can someone *not* need time to adjust? A 45-year-old I know whose father took his life decades ago was not able to talk about it openly until this year. And a friend of my wife's who lost her only daughter to multiple sclerosis still weeps over her at times, though it's been twenty years. Often, the ability to recover quickly turns out to be something else, like the ability to mask pain. And though it is "common sense" that time heals, it may not be true for everyone. For some, the pain of grief intensifies with time.

As for the popular notion of "closure," Bud, who lost his 23-year-old daughter Julie in the 1995 bombing of Oklahoma City's federal building, has this to say: "I can't handle that word – I get tired of hearing it. The first time someone asked me about closure was the day after Julie's burial. The day after! I was still in hell then. In a way, I still am. How can there ever be closure? A part of my heart is gone."

Alexis, a woman whose brother committed suicide, feels the same thirty years after the fact: "The pain is *still* there, and I wonder how I could have prevented it. Was it something I said or did?" Sometimes no outward gesture, no word of comfort or encouragement, no happy memory can erase the guilt a person feels.

In short, there is no "answer" to the riddle of grief. But there is such a thing as community, and the knowledge of those who have experienced its blessings that even if one person, alone, cannot hold up under the crushing weight of loss, the heaviest burden *can* be lifted, or at least lightened when it is shared.

And for those who are open to it, there is the comfort of knowing that while God may not shield us from hardship and pain, he has promised that he is close to all those who grieve. As Psalm 34 puts it, "The Lord is close to the brokenhearted; he saves those crushed in spirit, and those who despair."

19

Resurrection

When Johannes Brahms' great *Requiem* was first performed in 1867, audiences were astonished. Instead of having set to music the usual prayers for the dead, the composer had borrowed verses from scripture that speak of comfort and hope.

Now you have sorrow, yet I will see you again,
and your heart shall rejoice, and your joy
no man shall take from you.

As a mother comforteth her child,
so I shall comfort you.

I have labored and toiled, yet found rest.
So you, too, shall rest.

Artistically speaking, such lyrics showed Brahms' gift for breathing new life into an old form. But there was another, more significant dimension to it. Two years before, his mother had died, and in choosing words that addressed his grief, he found a creative outlet for it, and a measure of healing.

Having lost both my parents two decades ago, and still feeling the loss keenly at times, I doubt Brahms was able to "get over" his mother's death with a work of art. More probably, he went on mourning for years. Still, his *Requiem* reflects a truth that cannot be denied, even if there is no such thing as full closure. Though grief is a harsh, long-lasting reality, there is a greater reality to which sadness must ultimately yield, and that is hope.

Across all cultures, men and women have found consolation and courage in the belief that death is not the end, but that it is followed by another, better life to come. How this next life will come about and what form it will take are questions that have occupied the human race down the centuries – and the answers people have come up with for them would easily fill another book.

Generally speaking, the world's major religions all agree that though our bodies decompose and return to the earth, our souls are released to another plane, either returning to their source, or moving on to find another frame. As writer Clarence Bauman puts it, "Being non-physical, our psyche is not subject to decay, but is conserved within a larger infinite spiritual accountability.

Just as our decayed body is reabsorbed by this planet…
so our mental and spiritual components are transposed
into the realm that ultimately determines the origin and
destiny of all knowing and being."

Explaining the same process in different terms, my
grandfather, writer Eberhard Arnold, says that our flesh,
blood, and bones are not, in the truest and deepest sense,
our real selves. Being mortal, they die. Meanwhile the
real seat of our being, the soul, passes from mortality
into immortality, and from time into timelessness. It returns from the body it was breathed into back to its author, God. That is why, my grandfather says, the human
soul longs perpetually for God, and why, instead of
merely dying, we are "called into eternity" and reunited
with him.

For those of us who call ourselves Christians, it is
impossible to contemplate such a future without recalling the resurrection of Jesus, the "Son of Man," and the
price he paid for it – a harrowing public execution on a
Roman cross. After all, his death was not just an isolated
historical event, but (as he himself indicated by saying,
"Follow me") the unavoidable gateway through which
each of us must pass if we want to share everlasting life
with him. "Whoever tries to save his life will lose it, but
whoever loses it for my sake will find it."

To the extent that our paths must trace Christ's, the fear of death is not only understandable, but natural. He himself cried out in anguish, "My father, why have you forsaken me?" and begged him, "Let this cup pass me by." When I first heard the story of the crucifixion from my father, I could not stomach its cruelty, and everything in me rebelled. Why couldn't there be Easter without the horrors of Good Friday?

Over the years, however, I found an answer that I could accept: just as there can be no spring without the cold of winter that comes before it – just as the glory of a sunrise would be nothing if it did not break through the darkness of night – so the pain of suffering must precede the triumph of new life. In finding this faith, I gradually overcame my fear of dying.

Those who do not believe in a life beyond the grave sometimes dismiss the idea out of hand, and given our inability to describe the future, except in terms of vague hopes, this is understandable. But to a dying person who does have faith in resurrection, it is not just an abstraction. It is a source of courage and strength so real that it can even alter him physically. Sometimes it is a matter of something as simple as a smile; sometimes there is an unexpected burst of energy or the sudden return of mobility and speech. It is as if the dying one is standing on the threshold of eternity. Moments like these hint at the immortality of the soul – and the beauty that is still there in the most exhausted, decrepit body.

Poet William Blake, who was captivated by the themes of heaven, hell, time, and eternity throughout his life, said that to him dying would be no more than "moving from one room to another." According to his wife, this confidence remained with him in his final hours. He spent them lying in bed, weak but joyous, and singing one song after another.

The philosopher Søren Kierkegaard, who died at forty-three, met death with similar joy – and with the certainty that it was not just an end, but a beginning. His nephew wrote:

Never have I seen the spirit break through the earthly husk and impart to it such a glory…He took my hand in both of his – how small they were and thin and palely transparent – and said, "Thank you for coming, and now farewell." But these simple words were accompanied by a look the match of which I have never seen. It shone out from a sublime and blessed splendor that seemed to me to make the whole room light. Everything was concentrated in those eyes as the source of light and heartfelt love, the blissful dissolution of sadness, a penetrating clearness of mind, and a jesting smile.

Jabez, a 92-year-old my parents got to know in England during the Second World War, faced dying with a similar joy. There was another angle to it, however. According to my father, this white-bearded patriarch was unconcerned about himself; his sights were set on something much greater. Sitting in his chair and looking out over the ripening fields, he often spoke of God's great harvest to come, and the eternal glory that would then break in on earth. Here was a man who lived in daily expectation of the coming Kingdom.

It is rare to be given such breadth of vision, and to be so detached from the worries that tend to plague the dying. But even if our vision is limited, we need not spend our last days in anxiety and fear. Remembering the last ten days of her mother's life, which she spent at her bedside, writer Dorothy Day reminds us that as long as we hold on to the proverbial mustard seed of faith, we will be led through doubt and despair.

> To sit by a dying person and see their intentness on what is happening...It is a struggle, a fearful, grim, physical struggle, to breathe, to swallow, to live.
>
> It was hard to talk about dying, but every now and then we did. I told her we could no more imagine the life beyond the grave than a blind man could imagine colors. But we also talked about faith, and how, because our knowledge was like a bridge which comes to an end, so that it

does not reach the other shore, we must pray, "I believe, O God. Help thou my unbelief." A wonderful prayer, that.

And we must remember that for the faithful, dying does not mean that life is taken away, but that it is *changed*. For when our dwelling here is taken away, an everlasting home still awaits us in heaven.

In a way, it requires no great leap of faith to believe in the transformation Day speaks of. It may be miraculous, but it can still be seen all around us daily, in nature – in the emergence of a butterfly from what was once a caterpillar, or a sprout from what was once a rotting seed. As for the mysteries of the hereafter, they are not entirely closed to us either. Having witnessed the final moments of many dying people, I have sensed the nearness of another place – call it eternity, heaven, the kingdom of God, or whatever – and according to hospice workers and others quoted in the book *Final Gifts*, this is a common experience among those who provide end-of-life care.

> Dying people may see a bright light or another place. Some review their lives and come to a more complete understanding of life's meaning...They are frequently given glimpses into another world and those waiting in it. Although they provide few details, they speak with awe and wonder of the peace and beauty they see in this other place. They tell of talking with people we cannot see...people they have known or loved. They may even tell us when their deaths will occur.

Nick, whom I quoted in the previous chapter, says that as his brother Matt drew his last breaths, he was given such a glimpse, after becoming aware of another presence or dimension in the room:

> Right after Matt went, his wife said that she could hear music or something like it. She said it was like singing, but more of a loud rushing sound. It's funny, but I swear that when she said that, I listened and I could hear something too. It's brought me to a different level of thinking about everything. I think we're so much more interconnected with the other world, as you might call it, than we sometimes assume. We have our little plans and go on with our little lives, but there's always that connection.

Bound as we are by the limits of time and space, we can only guess at what such things might mean; as the Apostle Paul says, we can only see "through a glass darkly." All the same, an inkling of eternity can – as Nick found – change our worldview in a significant way, and remind us that heaven is not just "pie in the sky." It is a reality here and now, even if a mysterious one.

I opened this book with the story of my sister Marianne, who died when I was six. But that was not actually the first death in our family. Eight years earlier, my parents had lost another daughter, Emmy – their first child –

when she was three months old. The following notes from my mother's diary reveal the depths of her anguish. Yet they also reflect a deep trust in the promise of resurrection, and because of that I would like to close the book with them. Standing as a reminder that love is greater than fear, and life more powerful than death, they have always given me hope:

> The last few days of our baby's life were hard for us to bear, yet still great and powerful, and filled with promise because of the nearness of Christ. Each time we interceded for our little one and gathered ourselves inwardly, the powers of death withdrew, and she revived. Whereas before she lay apathetic and unresponsive, with half-open eyes, shallow breath, and a very weak pulse, now she would suddenly open her eyes, look at us, and cry, moving her hands and turning her head when she was touched...

> There was an atmosphere of love in her room that went out from her and filled the whole house, and united us in love to each other. We took turns watching her. It was a hard fight, and she struggled so valiantly, it seemed incredible that she was only a tiny baby...

> Just before the end she opened her eyes wide, wider than ever before. Then, with a clear, otherworldly gaze, she looked at both of us for a long time. There was no sorrow and no suffering left in those eyes, but a message from the other world – a message of joy. Her eyes were not dull

and clouded but bright and shining. She could not tell us anything in words, of course, but her eyes bore witness to heavenly splendor and to the unspeakable joy there is with Christ. With this gaze, our dear baby took leave of us. I shall never forget her radiant eyes.

Epilogue

It is clear that when a person dies, eternity knocks at his door. Yet doesn't it knock for each of us, all the time? If we are elderly or ill, this isn't hard to imagine. It is much harder for those of us who are in good health, or in the prime of life. Then we are far more likely to see death as a negative thing, and to push it away as an unwanted reminder that not every dream of a long, happy life comes true. But even if we push it away, we can never know, when we get up in the morning, whether we have decades in front of us, or only days.

Just weeks ago my 32-year-old niece Carmen, a second-grade teacher and mother of four, was busy balancing the demands of parenthood and work; in the meantime she's been diagnosed with multiple sclerosis, and can neither stand at a blackboard nor give her baby a bath. Just weeks ago she was playing her viola at my youngest daughter's wedding; now she is so weak she can barely raise her head. Given the nature of her illness, Carmen could be on her feet again soon. But she could also find herself wheelchair-bound for the rest of her life.

Then there's my cousin Ben, sixty-eight, who was recently stricken by cancer. It spread so aggressively that by the time he was diagnosed, both surgery and chemo were ruled out as ineffective options for treatment. Though stable at the moment and buying time with painkillers and hormone blockers, he could go downhill at any time – something he's painfully aware of, especially on bad days. At the same time he is generally so upbeat that one would never guess what he is dealing with privately: nausea, fevers, restless nights, and moments when the thought of being separated from his wife of forty years becomes too much to bear without tears.

Because of Ben's medical condition, he is daily forced to confront the thought of death – and, when it attacks him, the demon of fear. But even if someone like him is far more conscious of his mortality than you or I, aren't all of us equally fragile in God's eyes? Given the uncertainty of any life from one week to the next, shouldn't every illness, every death speak to us and challenge our complacency? As Joseph Conrad reminds us in *Lord Jim*, our days are numbered whether we like it or not, and there is "never time to say our last word – the last word of our love, or our desire, faith, remorse…"

To watch someone die is always a shaking experience. But death need not have the final word. And if it seems like it does, perhaps that is because we spend too much time focusing on our fear of it. Like animals frozen in the headlights of an oncoming vehicle, we are so mesmerized by death that we forget the promise of eternal life that follows it. Bonhoeffer rightly admonishes:

> We pay more attention to dying than to death. We're more concerned to get over the act of dying than to overcome death. Socrates mastered the art of dying; Christ overcame death as the last enemy. There is a real difference between the two things; the one is within the scope of human possibilities, the other means resurrection. It's not by virtue of *ars moriendi* – the art of dying – that a new and purifying wind can blow through our present world. Only the resurrection of Christ can bring that about. Here is the answer to Archimedes' challenge: "Give me somewhere to stand, and I will move the earth." If only a few people really believed that and acted on it in their daily lives, a great deal would be changed…That is what living in the light of resurrection means.

Bonhoeffer, a modern martyr who refused to bend his conscience to fit the demands of Hitler's Third Reich, went to the gallows fearlessly, and to me, these words contain a key to his boldness. They also contain a vital kernel of wisdom: the thought that the best way – the only way – to truly overcome the fear of death is to live life in such a way that its meaning cannot be taken away by death.

This sounds grandiose, but it is really very simple. It means fighting the impulse to live for ourselves, instead of for others. It means choosing generosity over greed. It also means living humbly, rather than seeking influence and power. Finally, it means being ready to die again and again – to ourselves, and to every self-serving opinion or agenda.

In Dickens's *Christmas Carol*, the bitter old accountant Scrooge provides a memorable illustration. Tight-fisted and grasping, he goes through life dragging a chain that he himself has forged, link by link, with each miserly deed. Having closed himself to human kindness, he lives in a universe so calculating and cold that no one escapes his suspicion. Before long he begins to despise himself and look for a way out of his misery. But he cannot find one. He is trapped – trapped in the prison of self. Worse, he is haunted at night by dreams of death and dreads its approach.

Then he changes. Loosened by those same dreams, the scales fall from his eyes, and he sees a way out: "It is time to make amends." No longer consumed with his own needs, he is free to love. And as he runs from one old acquaintance to another, he rediscovers the world around him with the unselfconscious happiness of a child.

Such happiness can be ours, too, if we live for love. By "love" I am not speaking simply of the emotion, nor of some grand, abstract ideal, but of the life-changing power Jesus speaks of when he says:

> I was hungry and you gave me food, I was thirsty and you gave me drink, I was a stranger and you welcomed me, I was naked and you clothed me, I was sick and you visited me, I was in prison and you came to me. (Mt. 25: 35–36)

Love is a tangible reality. Sometimes it is born of passion or devotion; sometimes it is a hard-won fruit, requiring work and sacrifice. Its source is unimportant. But unless we live for love, we will not be able to meet death confidently when it comes. I say this because I am certain that when our last breath is drawn and our soul meets God, we will not be asked how much we have accomplished. We will be asked whether we have loved enough. To quote John of the Cross, "In the evening of life you shall be judged on love."

As my great-aunt Else lay dying of tuberculosis, a friend asked her if she had one last wish. She replied, "Only to love more." If we live our lives in love, we will know peace at the hour of death. And we will not be afraid.

Index of Names

Aaron 73
Abraham (Hebrew patriarch) 131
Adela 95
Alexis 185
Alice 35
Ann 41, 47
Anne 136
Antonetta, Susanne 17
Archimedes 199
Arnold, Eberhard 189
Arnold, Emmy ("Oma") 10, 93
Barry 130
Bauman, Clarence 125, 188
Ben 198
Bernall, Brad and Misty 49, 183
Bernall, Cassie 49, 183
Bernard 157
Blake, William 191
Blumhardt, Christoph 72
Bonhoeffer, Dietrich 199
Brahms, Johannes 187
Bronwen 87
Bud 185
Buxton, Ed 118
Callanan, Maggie 166
Carmen 197
Carmichael, Amy 82
Carole 46
Chuck 110
Conrad, Joseph 199
Dan 83
Day, Dorothy 192
Deb 114
Delf 181
Dickens, Charles 200
Dorie 18
Dorli 34

Dostoevsky, F. 29, 114
Doug 41, 47
Eddie 34
Edith 140
Eileen 157
Ellen 57
Elliott, Elisabeth 107
Emmy 194
Epperly, Bruce 122
Esther 162
Evelyn 79
Fran 112
Fred 71
Gabriel 35
Gareth 67
Gertrude 127
Gina 172
Greg 119
Gus 166
Hammarskjöld, Dag 145
Hannah 81
Hans 160
Hardy 91, 140
Herman 126, 164
Hillary 77
Hitler, Adolf 200
Irma 151
Isaac (Hebrew patriarch) 131
Isaiah (baby) 132
Jabez 192
Jackson, Jimmie Lee 6
James 64
Jane 37
Jarius 77
Jeremiah (Hebrew prophet) 29
Jim 25
Joan 153

Joel 102
John 67
John of the Cross 201
John Paul II xv
Jones, W. Paul 177
Judge, Father Mychal xvi
Julie 185
Justin 63
Kafka 26
Karen 81
Karl 150
Kathleen 125
Kathy 60, 180
Katie 73
Kierkegaard, S. 191
King, Martin Luther, Jr. 6
Kingsolver, Barbara 107
Lewis, C. S. 108, 146
Linda 43, 183
Lindbergh, Anne M. 174
Lisa 100
Liz 70
Luther, Martin 72
Lynn 63
Macdonald, George 40
Margaret 71
Margrit 158
Marianne 1, 194
Marjorie 180
Mark 169
Mark John 53
Mary 50
Matt 13, 43, 175, 183, 194
Maureen 161
McDonald, Steven xvii
Merrill 120, 180
Mike, Father xvi
Miriam 105
Monika 5
Mother Teresa 123, 152
Muggeridge, Malcolm 124

Myra 173
Nick 176, 194
Nouwen, Henri 170, 183
Oyler, Chris 179
Pat 90
Paul (the Apostle) 23
Pete 50
Polycarp 128
Prejean, Helen 167
Rachel 65
Rachoff, Vassili 4
Ramona 130
Randy 175
Ray 94
Rick 70
Rilla 61
Ruby 41, 47
Scrooge 200
Sergei 96
Sheila 25
Shirley 73
Sibyl 67
Sidney 180
Simon 142
Socrates 199
Solzhenitsyn, A. 108
Spragins, Ellyn 182
Stephen 34
Terkel, Studs 173
Terry 23
Tina 91
Tolstoy, Leo 38, 139
Tom 172
Travis 78
von Hollander, Else 202
Wendell 51
Winifred 60
Xaverie 67
Yancey, Philip 163
Zach 147

Also by Johann Christoph Arnold

Why Forgive?
ISBN 1-57075-512-4

In *Why Forgive?* the reader will meet men and women
who have earned to the right to talk about the importance of overcoming hurt—and about the peace of
mind they have found in doing so. Why forgive? Read
these stories, and then decide.
ISBN 1-57075-512-4

Eberhard Arnold
*Writings Selected with an Introduction by
Johann Christoph Arnold*
ISBN 1-57075-304-0

Eberhard Arnold, founder of the Bruderhof, was one of
the most remarkable Christian figures of the twentieth
century. In the years after World War I he abandoned
his career as an academic theologian to live by the rad-
ical spirit of the Sermon on the Mount. His writings,
which concern the quest for peace, community, and the
call to a revolution of the spirit, ring with the inspiring
challenge to live as if the Gospel were true.

Available from Orbis Books
Maryknoll, NY 10545-0308

Call 1-800-258-5838
or visit our website at www.orbisbooks.com

Thank you for reading *Be Not Afraid*.
We hope you enjoyed it.